THE EARLY DAYS
OF THE LITTLE MONK

The Seventh Gift

BY HARRY FARRA
illustrated by Christopher Fay

PAULIST PRESS
New York and Mahwah, N.J.

Cover design by Morris Berman Studio

Library of Congress Cataloging-in-Publication Data

Farra, Harry.
    The early days of the little monk : the seventh gift / by Harry Farra ; illustrated by Christopher Fay.
        p.   cm.
    ISBN 0–8091–3875–1 (alk. paper)
    I. Title.
PS3556.A738 E2 1999
813′.54—dc21   99–23354
                                                                          CIP

Published by Paulist Press
997 Macarthur Boulevard
Mahwah, New Jersey 07430

www.paulistpress.com

Printed and bound in the
United States of America

Contents

iv Contents

ACKNOWLEDGMENTS

Quotations of François Fénelon based on his *Spiritual Letters* are used by permission of Whitaker House, 30 Hunt Valley Circle, New Kensington, Pa. 15068, from their book *Let Go*, copyright © 1973 by Banner Publishing.

Permission was granted by the Church Hymnal Corporation for use of a collect from *The Book of Common Prayer* and for a hymn, "I Sing a Song of the Saints of God," from *The Hymnal 1982*.

The words about silence by Gerard Manley Hopkins are from his poem "The Habit of Perfection," which appeared in *The Poems of Gerard Manley Hopkins* by W. H. Gardner and N.H. Mackenzie, Oxford University Press, New York, copyright © 1967.

Paulist Press has given permission for the passage about the hazelnut, which comes from the fifth chapter of *Julian of Norwich: Showings*, translated by Edmund Colledge, O.S.A., and James Walsh, S.J., copyright © 1978 (Classics of Western Spirituality Series).

Quotations from St. Benedict come from *The Rule of St. Benedict*, translated by Anthony C. Meisel and M. L. del Mastro, a Doubleday Image book, copyright © 1975. Used by permission.

Quotations of Brother Lawrence are taken from *The Practice of the Presence of God*, Fleming H. Revell Co., Westwood, N.J., copyright © 1958.

"The Princess with the Glass Heart" is based on a story of that title by Richard Leander and translated by Anna Eichberg as it appeared in *St. Nicholas* magazine, 1883.

Scripture quotations marked (TEV) are from the Today's English Version—Second Edition, copyright © 1992 by American Bible Society. Used by permission.

Scripture quotations marked (NRSV) are from the New Revised Standard Version Bible, copyright © 1989, by the

Division of Christian Education of the National Council of the Churches of Christ in the United States of America. Used by permission.

Several sources need special acknowledgment:

The story of the fox in the chapter "At Home in the Universe" is based on an event in the life of Loren Eiseley as described in his book *The Star Thrower*, Times Books, copyright © 1987.

The story of the musicians in the chapter "To Whom Should I Give My Money?" is based on an anecdote by Meredith Wilson, composer of *The Music Man*, and appeared in the liner notes for the sound track, Warner Brothers Records, 1962.

The shepherd's story in the chapter "The Shepherd's Return" has its origins in the title of a contemporary African American spiritual, "Soon and Very Soon."

The idea for the extremists in spiritual disciplines in the chapter "The Zeal of Gorbon Kreeg" came from a short story of Franz Kafka titled "The Hunger Artist."

My gratitude goes out again to my colleague and mentor S. S. Hanna, who never fails to inspire me to greater heights of productivity.

My wife, Vonnie, has been there faithfully for me doing the hard work of typing, editing and proofing.

My debt to Father Boadt continues to grow with each new book of mine falling under his creative eye and wise judgment.

I was delighted when Christopher Fay agreed to do the illustrations for this second "little monk" book as well.

DEDICATION

To
Charles R. Reed
who loves life,
treasures good ideas,
stirs deep discussions
and serves Jesus Christ with courage and integrity.

Lectio Divina (Meditative Reading That Leads to Prayer)

God plants the seeds of a monk in everyone's soul at
the moment of creation.
—Frank Bianco, *Voices of Silence*

> Lord, I have given up my pride,
> and turned from my arrogance.
> I am not concerned with great matters,
> or with subjects too difficult for me.
> Instead, I am content and at peace.
> As a child lies quietly in its mother's arms,
> so my heart is quiet within me.
> Israel, trust in the Lord,
> now and forever.
> —Psalm 131 TEV

> I ask no dream, no prophet ecstasies,
> No sudden rending the veil of clay,
> No angel visitant, no op'ning skies,
> But take the dimness of my soul away.
> —"Spirit of God, Descend upon My Heart,"
> George Croly, 1854

These words the Lord spoke with a loud voice to your whole assembly at the mountain, out of the fire, the cloud, and the thick darkness and he added no more. He wrote them on two stone tablets, and gave them to me. When you heard the voice out of the darkness, while the mountain was burning with fire, you approached me, all the heads of your tribes and your elders; and you said, "Look, the Lord our God has shown us his glory and greatness, and we have heard his voice out of the fire. Today we have seen that God may speak to someone and the person may still live. So now why should we die? For this great fire will consume us; if we hear the voice of the Lord our God any longer, we shall die. For who is there of all flesh that has heard the voice of the living God speaking out of the fire, as we have, and remained alive? Go near, you yourself, and hear all that the Lord our God will say. Then tell us everything that the Lord our God tells you, and we will listen and do it."

—Deuteronomy 5:22–27 *NRSV*

> And so I find it well to come
> For deeper rest to this still room,
> For here the habit of the soul
> Feels less the outer world's control;
> The strength of mutual purpose pleads
> More earnestly our common needs;
> And from the silence multiplied
> By these still forms on either side,
> The world that time and sense have known
> Falls off and leaves us God alone.
>
> —"The Meeting," John Greenleaf Whittier

1. First You Enter a Narrow Gate

The Feast of St. Augustine, early in the little monk's sojourn at the monastery in Maloo, the city of God.

The land smelled of sheep dung and new-mown hay.

The little monk sat on a stone bench in the novices' garden. Since a monk's hands are not to be idle, he whittled away at a thin, infant limb from a walnut tree. He often made tiny carved animals or whistles for the children of the valley.

During such times, his mind centered itself on God. Yet no particular thoughts formed there today, no real images, no special feelings. His mind rested simply in the presence of God.

Then a questioning prayer stirred: Lord Jesus, will I find you here? I've crossed an ocean to find you. Where are you? Where will I find you? Are you in the chapel? Are you in the kitchen? I've looked in the refectory, in the scriptorium, even in the orchard and the cemetery. I've waited in this beautiful garden, too. If I can't find you, will you find me? When will you come to me? Where?

Two copper beech trees formed a leafy arch over the garden. The little monk sat quietly and prayerfully on the stone bench, looking like a garden statue frozen in marble and alabaster, calling pilgrims to devotion.

The little monk yielded himself to the serenity of the day. A friendly bird landed on the bench beside him, took some

1

"A monk's hands are not to be idle..."

seeds from his hand and then began to sing. All creatures of the earth praise the Creator in their own way, thought the little monk. What is my way? he mused.

He started to meditate on the words from one of the hymns of Morning Prayer: "All creatures of our God and King, lift up your voices, let us sing."

Beyond the singing of the bird, an Angelus bell tolling softly in the distance and the nattering of young goats on a faraway hill of purple heather, nothing seemed out of place in this magic mural. The whole creation surrendered itself to a moment as hushed as a library, as quiet as a museum, as peaceful as an empty tomb.

Near the ivy-covered wall, the garden gate creaked suddenly on its hinges from a visit of the wind. Usually, when contemplating God, the little monk's mind pushed away all distractions by the simple joy of being in God's presence. But, the ominous sound of the gate opening stirred some apprehension in him. To him, gates were mystical messengers.

He remembered the conversation with his mother the day he left home in search of Maloo. "Mother, what will happen to me there? What will I do?" he had asked. "First, you enter a narrow gate," she replied, filling the words with special significance. That's all she said. When pressed for more, she said nothing beyond repeating, "First, you enter a narrow gate."

His mind let go of God for the moment now in order to grasp the growing image of the garden gate and therefore, all the gates of life. Nothing of purpose or consequence, he thought, ever gets done without first entering a narrow gate.

Gates lead to decisions. The main events of life are marked by narrow gates. To enter life we come through the gate of the womb. To enter school, we go through a narrow gate. The gate in front of the church reminds all who pass by of the narrow gate to heaven. The cemetery that waits for us all at the end of the road is guarded by a high fence and an iron gate. All sorts of mysteries hide behind the narrow gates, he decided.

Then, the little monk remembered the words of Jesus as Matthew recorded them in his gospel journal: "Enter by the narrow gate, since the road that leads to destruction is wide and spacious, and many take it; but it is a narrow gate and a hard road that leads to life, and only few find it."

The little monk returned in his mind to an earlier time in his childhood when his mother led him off to school the very first day. As they walked the three miles to school, the young lad saw hints in each shift of scene that meant a dramatic change in his life from that day forward. Friendly merchants called from the porches of their stores, "So, you're off to school today." "Who's his teacher?" shouted a mother from a kitchen window. The tone of her voice said, I'm with you; I've gone through this many times. "Miss Graham," his mother reported. "He'll be in good hands then," hollered the woman, turning back into the kitchen to finish the apple pies she had left for a moment.

In front of the school, while the school bell rang out its authority over the children of the world, his mother took his hand from hers and placed it in the teacher's hand. What is this? he thought. Am I being given away? he wondered. As the teacher led him through the school gate, he looked over his shoulder to see his mother hurrying down the street. Something happened that day. Something tore in the seamless robe that held mother and son together in a special bond of love. Life never seemed the same after walking through that gate. Mystery, awe and fear—all lay in the haze behind the narrow gate.

Then his mind focused on cemeteries. When one passes through that gate, everything is left behind—possessions, family, friends, relatives, dreams and plans. For that last journey, we leave even our flesh behind like some discarded garment.

Now the little monk ambled over to the garden gate to examine it. Thorns from nearby bushes had scraped sharp lines into the paint on the gate.

Purr, as cats are wont to do, slept peacefully beneath one of the rose bushes on a bed of soft, red petals.

Shielding his eyes from a patch of sun, the little monk squinted at the white slats of the garden gate, trying to grasp the fuller meaning of this back gate into the world of the monastery. "Behind every door hides either an opportunity or a warning," his mother had told him several times. The poet within him fashioned these words:

> Tiny gate by the garden great,
>   Why do you make me choose,
> Between the mystery within
>   And the uncertainty without?
> To risk a world, or a world lose?

The little monk had a peculiar thing in his fundamental makeup—he often thought in poetry. His natural mind seemed bent toward rhythm and rhyme. "While others think in prose, my son thinks in poetry and song," the little monk's mother often explained about this wrinkle in his mind.

A different set of memories came rushing back of the first day the little monk arrived at the monastery of Maloo. He came to the front gate wearied and unsure. He stood for a long time at that iron gate, wrestling with the deep issues of his calling—the far greater promise of eternal glory overshadowing the possible pleasures of this world. He put his hand to the gate. He could feel the rust beneath the many layers of paint.

He turned to leave and took a step or two, but then stopped. His heart told him to stay. He looked above the door to where some ancient craftsman had carved a single word in Latin into the stone—*"Obsculta!"* He rubbed his eyes with the knuckles of his hands, hoping that if he saw the Latin more clearly, he would understand it. "Listen," the Spirit whispered to him. How simple, how profound, how hard just to listen, thought the little monk.

Finally he slid the bolt in the heavy gate and walked to the door of the monastery. For a time he stood still, paralyzed in indecision. What am I doing here? he thought. This is no place for a person like me. Surely God must be laughing that I should think I could be a monk of Maloo. He reached down and touched the first knot on the prayer rope around his waist. "Lord Jesus Christ, Son of God, be merciful to me, a sinner," he prayed. Then, following the custom of most monasteries, he knocked loudly at the door three times before someone answered, "Who is it?"

"The little monk," he called out to the one who questioned him from behind the closed door.

"What do you want?" asked the voice.

"To join the community and learn to pray without ceasing," answered the little monk timidly. A long silence followed. The monastic community always gave a seeker time to weigh this most serious decision.

In his long journey from England to Maloo, he had seen the world and found it wanting.

He came to Maloo to do spiritual battle, armed with a few simple weapons—a journal; his cat, Purr; and a leather sling.

A child gave him the sling when he left the cathedral under orders from the bishop to go in search of Maloo and the prayer without ceasing.

On arriving at the monastery in Maloo, the little monk had surrendered his cat, his journal and his sling to the leaders of

"The little monk started to swing freely on the gate…"

the monastery. But, they told him, "Tie that sling to your waist and if you ever see the Devil, sling your best stones at him—one for Adam, one for Eve and one for Jesus. As for Purr, she may enter, too. Maloo's a place that welcomes cats as well as holy monks." The leaders conversed quietly among themselves, then added, "You may keep your journal—for now. But remember this, what you write cannot be erased. For, what you first write comes straight from the heart. A journal is worthless unless it is true."

Now, as a student in the Lord's service, the little monk stood at the rear gate, the garden gate, and reflected further on the mystery of narrow gates.

He climbed on the gate, his feet resting on the bottom board. The gate creaked a small warning, then yielded itself to those innocent feet. The little monk started to swing freely on the gate, his robe billowing in the breeze. The gate surrendered to this holy intruder and squeaked cheerfully as the little monk threw back his head with his face toward the sky. He swung and swung and swung on the friendly gate.

His heart longed for the gift of contemplation. Purr yawned and laid her head back down on the bed of petals. Sleep comes easily to contented cats.

The little monk heard a slight swish in the ivy that formed itself into a great green hand holding the monastery in its palm, offering up to God all that the monastery contained.

Are you in the garden here, Jesus? the little monk wondered.

2. The Shepherd's Visit

*U*nnoticed by the little monk, something else stirred in the bushes nearby. Unheard by the little monk, a voice whispered: "It's him. The Promise said, 'A child shall swing on the gates of eternity.' That's him. That's what the Promise meant."

Suddenly, a strange coolness touched the little monk's skin.

Everything around him fell into a deeper silence. Even the usually lively birds went into a hush. A hidden presence filled the garden like a mist of rain or fog rolling in quietly from the sea. A twig snapped behind the little monk. He turned too quickly, and thorns from the roses scratched his legs, opening a small wound.

But he was too frightened to notice.

In the bushes, the long blur of a shadow appeared. Cautiously, the little monk moved toward the place of the shadow. The smell of garlic and dirty animals spilled out of the bushes. "Come out," commanded the little monk, shaking all the way down to his sandals.

A tall, gaunt man with ragged clothes came out of the bushes. His battered cap looked as if he did not belong to this world. The foul odor from tending sheep hung on his clothes, and garlic spewed from his mouth whenever he breathed or spoke.

"Who are you?" asked the little monk.

"Just an old shepherd. No one to do you harm," answered the strange figure in the garden.

*"Purr lifted her sleepy head and saw a lamb
hidden in the bushes…"*

"What do you want?" asked the little monk, not sure what he had encountered here.

"To give you something," said the shepherd.

"Give me something?" queried the little monk, holding the edge of the gate and tipping his head to the side.

"Something that you need," the shepherd said.

"I need nothing," the little monk answered honestly.

"Someday you might," said the shepherd. The little monk sensed a warning in the words.

"No, truly, I need nothing but God." That sounded a little arrogant thought the little monk. An awkward pause followed the little monk's comment. I shouldn't allow this person too far into my life, the little monk noted to himself. The shepherd's eyes saw more than the little monk wanted him to see.

"Whose cat is that?" asked the shepherd, breaking the silence.

"She's mine—and God's," he thought he should add. He never liked having too many questions about his cat. He stepped to the side to put himself between the shepherd and the cat.

"Where did you get her?" asked the shepherd.

"In an old crate in a back alley," said the little monk cautiously. "She was one of the wounded of the world—starving, orphaned and battle-scarred."

"Have you named her?" asked the shepherd, who knew all of his sheep by name and disposition, from the youngest to the oldest.

"Her name's Purr," he said, hoping the questions would end. The soul has a natural aversion to questions, he remembered writing in his journal one time. Purr lifted her sleepy head. She saw a lamb hidden in the bushes, peering out at her. In a remarkable moment, innocence stared at innocence. Purr twitched her ears and the lamb retreated into the bushes.

The little monk felt obligated to add: "I called her that because of the soft, peaceful purr she gives off when she's centered down into herself. It's her own chant of praise, a hymn of contentment."

"Who are you?" asked the shepherd.

"I'm the little monk," he answered, closing the narrow gate to the garden. "I came here to fulfill the command of the apostle Paul to be 'devoted to prayer.'"

"Why Maloo?" asked the shepherd.

"Because my bishop in England sent me here to learn to pray without ceasing." The little monk did not enjoy this inquisition.

"How did you get here?" queried the shepherd.

"I came by a long journey, an odyssey of hope—first as a lowly potter, then as a monk of God," answered the little monk.

The little monk turned away from the questioning eyes that kept him under surveillance.

A pause.

"But what are you really here for?" asked the little monk, still nervous about his encounter with the shepherd.

"Because of the gift," replied the shepherd.

"I don't know what you mean," said the little monk. But the shepherd was long on patience.

"All of us, sometime in our life, need a special gift," answered the shepherd.

"I still don't understand," said the little monk.

"Well, it happened to me," said the shepherd. He had a habit of pointing his finger at your heart when trying to impart some wisdom to you. In his other hand he clasped a rugged staff made from a gnarled limb of an ancient tree. To the little monk, it looked more like a club than a staff.

"The shepherd turned back a final time, lifted his gnarled staff to the sky and called to him, 'I will come again, little monk.'"

"I really don't need anything," replied the little monk as forcefully as he could under the circumstance.

"Perhaps not now," said the shepherd. "But I will come again, little monk. Perhaps you'll need the gift then." The shepherd's eyes narrowed into a seriousness the little monk had rarely seen before in anyone else. "In the meantime, beware of Gorbon Kreeg."

"Who's Gorbon Kreeg?" asked the little monk nervously, looking down at a spider crossing over his toes. He shook off the spider.

"Never mind. Gorbon Kreeg will make himself known to you soon enough. Remember, little monk, beware the whispers of Gorbon Kreeg."

That said, the shepherd turned and headed off toward the distant hills. The little monk watched until the shepherd's figure almost faded into the clouds gathering near the top of Mount Maloo.

The shepherd turned back a final time, lifted his gnarled staff to the sky and called to him, "I will come again, little monk."

The fierceness of this prophecy worried the little monk. But then, he shook off the strange encounter as one of little significance. He took off his sandals and smacked the soles together to knock off the sand.

Then, barefoot, he returned to swinging on the waiting gate. His mind filled easily with treasured thoughts of England. How he loved dear old England. He thought of the legend that as a youth Jesus had traveled to England with Joseph of Arimathaea, who owned tin mines there. The little monk remembered how William Blake had immortalized this legend with these words:

And did those feet in ancient time
  Walk upon England's mountains green?
And was the holy Lamb of God
  On England's pleasant pastures seen?

In the midst of these hallowed memories, his eye caught sight of something on the stone bench, near where Purr had her own dreams going. He slipped off the swinging gate and went over to the bench, where he found a large hazelnut. He looked around to see where it might have come from, then decided it had been left by a forgetful squirrel.

He held the hazelnut in the palm of his hand, gazing at its beauty, but not knowing the truth it contained for him.

One of the hinges on the gate snapped in two. As the gate fell, a corner of the gate dug a gash in the earth. Purr awakened from her sleep with a fright. The little monk surveyed the damaged hinge. This gate is going to take a lot of work, he concluded.

3. Silence Is Your Friend

"In silence is the beginning of all things," said Servant Jonathan.

"A grain of wheat is born again in the deep quiet of the earth. The wind waits in the four corners of silent space before being called into action. Flowers grow without making a sound," he said, holding up a colorful marigold from the meadow.

The little monk had only just begun to know and appreciate the call to stillness that surrounds the monastery.

But even in a monastery, silence often has to give way to another full day of worship and work from the hand of God.

Morning Prayer yielded itself to the more earthly endeavor of breakfast. The Great Silence that rules the monastery every evening and night broke with the shuffle of chairs being pulled up to the breakfast table.

After a bleak meal of lumpy oats, day-old bread and strong, black tea, someone motioned to the little monk. Time had come for some instruction by the director of the novices.

All of the novices gathered in a plain and simple room still fresh and clean from the morning's mopping and dusting of it. Each monk at Maloo had a few basic things—a Bible, a breviary of prayers, psalms and hymns, *The Rule of St. Benedict* and a bucket and rag for serving others through cleaning the monastery floors, walks and walls.

"Listen to your bucket."

"Of these five tools of holiness," the abbot had told them in his homily on the first day of their arrival at Maloo, "the one most likely to prepare your soul finally for being a true monk will be your bucket. Listen to your bucket. It will purge your soul of the things of this world, the things that great men count important. Listen to your bucket. It will teach you humility, the first discipline." The little monk held his bucket to his chest and stared into it, looking for meaning.

The abbot, Servant Jonathan, continued: "This bucket and rag will become the basin and towel by which you will humbly kneel and wash the feet of the world." The little monk thought of Jesus bending to wash the feet of his disciples at the Last Supper.

"Oh God, give the heart of a learner and the ear of a disciple to these seekers of the deeper life," prayed Brother Stephen, the novice master. "Help them to climb to the last rung of the ladder of prayer."

Brother Stephen gave a word of daily business. "Some of you are quite new to this area. If you ever get lost, always remember the cluster of three trees in the middle of the woods, by the clearing. Those three trees—holly, evergreen and oak—always have been a landmark, a compass for the people who live here. The people call it Prophets' Point. 'It's a visual hymn to the character of God,' one old-timer told us long ago.

"Another villager told us, 'The trees look like the prophets Abraham, Moses and Elijah. But sometimes they transform themselves into the face of God.' You can see how that spot has legend to it. No matter where you are, if you look across the tops of the trees, you will see some key point of the land.

"If you're ever in doubt, ask the children. The children know. They play there all the time, regardless of the season. The children say that standing in the middle of the triangle formed by those prophetic trees creates magical power."

The novices all looked at each other to see if they should take this idea seriously. Even the novice master had a special twinkle in his eye. "Benedict always insists that we not take ourselves too seriously in this serious work of praise and holiness," Servant Jonathan, the abbot, had told them early on.

"We wish to speak today about the rule of silence, the supreme tool for shaping you like Christ," said Brother Stephen, looking keenly at the new crop of unlikely would-be monks. "Silence is the greatest gift a monastery can offer you. Monks are not born monks, but are hammered that way on the anvil of silence.

"Brother Sigmund will teach you the rule of silence. Later on, down the road of your instruction, Brother Egan will talk to you about that other great treasure of monastic life—mindfulness."

Brother Sigmund walked to the podium. This handsome, husky man could command attention just by his sheer presence in a room.

The little monk rubbed his hands together in anticipation of secrets being shared, of things being unlocked from eternity's edge, of hidden mysteries being revealed. His eyes narrowed into deep concentration. This is the moment you've been waiting for, his heart told him. He remembered a few lines scrawled in heavy ink in his journal—words of the poet, Gerard Manley Hopkins:

> Elected Silence, sing to me
> And beat upon my whorlèd ear,
> Pipe me to pastures still and be
> The music that I care to hear.

Brother Sigmund began his presentation about silence: "God himself dwells in silence. He is the friend of silence.

He does his best work in silence. Silence releases the healing power of the universe. There is a wonderful passage in the book called Wisdom, telling of the way in which the Word itself came rushing out of silence: '...while all things were in peaceful silence and the night was swift in her course, your Almighty Word leaped down from heaven out of your royal throne.'

"The Quakers wrote of three kinds of silence—sifting, sorting, stripping—that bring our souls naked before the God in whose presence all things become transparent.

"One of the church's great calls to worship is the beautiful text from Habakkuk: 'The Lord is in his holy temple: let all the earth keep silence before him.' Do you recall, also, that they built Solomon's Temple in silence? We're told in the Book of Kings that 'there was neither hammer nor ax nor any tool of iron heard in the house while it was being built.'

"Heaven itself, amid songs of victory and shouts of triumph, is a place where silence often fills the city of God. In one of his heavenly visions, the apostle John described this scene: 'When the Lamb opened the seventh seal, there was silence in heaven for about half an hour.'"

The little monk wrote down these wise words in his journal as carefully as a scribe copying scripture. Then he placed his hand, palm down, over the words and offered a brief prayer: "O God, Shepherd of Israel, make me a faithful pilgrim in the journey to silence."

A bird landed on the windowsill, did a funny dance, folded its wings, nuzzled its head under one wing and slipped into a late morning nap, oblivious to the import of the lecture that day. The little monk watched the bird's humorous ritual, a tiny clown on matchstick legs. Some things are created by God to be silly to remind us of our

"A bird landed on the windowsill and did a funny dance."

own folly and to show us our need of humility, thought the little monk.

Then he admired the trust of this small creature of a big universe. I can barely see it breathe, thought the little monk. A verse of scripture came to him, one about "waiting on the Lord." He saw some meaning in this: Wait upon the Lord, as quietly, patiently and trustfully as a sleeping bird on a summer day.

At that moment, his ears caught the closing words of Brother Sigmund's presentation. "Remember, silence is the canvas on which the Holy Spirit paints his truth for your soul. Learn to center down into that silence. Silence is the greatest tool for exposing us to the voice of God. The ultimate goal is not silence of the lips, but silence of the heart.

"In a moment, we will go into silence. When we do, reach out your hand and see if you can touch the silence. Sift it like a farmer taking a fistful of wheat and letting it run through his fingers. When you can taste it, smell it, touch it, breathe it, you will have found the creative spark of the universe—silence. When you can reach out and touch the silence, you will be a true monk."

The novices waited for the silence. They reached out to touch it, but they felt nothing but the skin of their fingers rubbing together.

Many of them were disappointed at their first attempt to learn the power of silence. "Don't worry about this," Brother Sigmund said. "It's not whether you grasp silence but whether silence grasps you.

"Silence and listening are gifts of God to be found at the end of much patient and persistent practice. Learn to listen in winter to the monastery pop and groan on its foundations. Listen to the walls whisper stories to each other. Listen to the stones cry out. Listen to the summer grass murmur in the wind. Listen to the gate creak. These things will train you to listen to God.

"This is a hard saying, I know. But listening to the silence, dwelling in solitude, surrendering to the still point within you—that's what will finally turn you into the Lord's prophet."

The little monk looked in the direction of the bird on the sill. It stood on one leg with its head tipped sideways, as if to say, why are you making so much of listening? We do it every day, sitting among the leaves of the trees, cradled by the wind.

Brother Sigmund continued. "Silence permeates our life here at Maloo. In silence we can finally learn to listen to the heart of God. If you violate the rule of silence, you do violence to another's soul as well as your own. The psalmist said it best: 'Make your soul wait in the Lord's leisure.'"

He whispered the words so that one had to strain to listen to them. Then he closed with a question, "What is the very first word in *The Rule of St. Benedict,* that rule by which we live here together?"

None of the novices remembered the answer. Brother Sigmund did not tell them.

One by one, without a sound, each novice looked around awkwardly, not knowing what to do. Then each humbled form got up to leave. By habit of the heart and the rhythm of daily life and worship at the monastery, they all headed off to the chapel. They sat in the "nobodies'" section, called that because these monks were new, undeveloped in their walk with God, but also because they were seeking to live obscure lives, to disappear into God like all good monks.

Sunlight spilled through stained-glass windows, which shattered the light into rainbow shards and shadows. The first psalm rose to life. The little monk closed his eyes during the singing and fell into dreamy contemplation.

Then, a bright, cheerful hymn filled the chapel with its joy and pierced the day. The little monk paid little attention until certain words and phrases rang in his mind. Between song and silence, he heard the words as if they were raindrops on a tin roof, each one a staccato sound. The high theology of this great hymn described God as "light inaccessible hid from our eyes." And that God was "unresting, unhasting and silent as light."

The abbot spoke briefly to the novices. "Go to your cells. Your cells will teach you all things—especially to listen."

The little monk entered his cell and shut the door tightly. He looked at what the stark room held: a straw bed, a small nightstand, a study table and a hard chair, so old that Abraham and Moses could have owned it. He went over to the worn nightstand by his bed and picked up his copy of *The Rule of St. Benedict*, given to him the first day he walked through the narrow gate to the monastery and knocked on its door, begging entrance. The book fell open easily to the first page. A single word, the first word, caught his eye. The Latin letters stood at attention, *"Obsculta!"* "Listen!" The very words carved over the main door to the monastery.

Later that night, the little monk climbed into his straw-bottomed bed. He cupped his hands behind his head and peered into the empty darkness of his room. The haunting lines of the hymn that day came back for a visit: "Oh, help us to see 'tis only the splendor of light hideth Thee."

Toward midnight he turned on his side to stare at the stars. He noticed a patch of soft moonlight near his stone pillow. He reached out to touch the light. Just as he could not touch the silence, neither could he touch the light.

"Silent as light," he mumbled to himself as he drifted off again into trustful sleep.

Later that night, he awoke in the middle of the Great Silence. He lay there listening to the cold, lonely and empty silence. Then he opened the door of his cell and stepped into a hallway that had become a long river of peacefulness. Purr followed him on soft, silent feet. He remembered what one of the monks had told him about the Great Silence: "It penetrates even the pores of your skin and goes down into your bones. It's a good silence, a healing silence. Some mornings you don't even want to bathe for fear of washing away the healing balm of silence."

But the little monk's own sandals broke the silence as he tiptoed along the hall. Then he returned to his cell. At the study table, he wrote in his journal, "O God, let me walk in your silence with the soft feet of a cat."

Purr climbed onto the little monk's lap. The little monk realized that Purr had learned not to meow during the Great Silence. In learning silence so quickly, Purr is a better monk than I, concluded the little monk. He closed his journal on the table and settled into bed, stroking Purr's fur until she went to sleep.

Soon the whole land bowed itself down to the dark heart of night.

The little monk's dreams set sail on a sea of silence, except for an occasional hoarse snore or gasping snort from one of the other monks down the hall, turning restlessly on the large stones they used for pillows.

4. We All Have a Monk in Our Heart

*B*ad news travels slowly in a monastery—and sometimes not at all. Only one topic ever moved swiftly from cell to cell, monk to monk—someone leaving the monastery for good. By a coded glance of the eyes, a gesture of the hand, a shrug of the shoulder, the whole community knew. They knew.

Not long into the little monk's days at Maloo, a particular monk, Brother Edward, did go back into the world. The decision to leave came from that monk's meeting with the abbot. Both were in agreement that Brother Edward did not have the calling to spend his life in a monastery. And, according to the monastic rule, the monk had to leave within the hour.

He could speak to no one, not even the brother sent to help him make his preparations for reentering the world. Nothing that he had as a monk really belonged to him—his robe, his sandals, his prayer book, his cleaning bucket or *The Rule of St. Benedict.* These were all on loan from God and the community. He put them into an orderly pile no larger than two loaves of bread side by side and left them behind.

He put on the same suit of clothes he had worn to the monastery. By custom, they hung in a small closet for several years until the monk made a final vow to the community or left the monastery. In a simple ceremony, the monk ready to profess his vows would be led to a table on which lay his old garments and the new garb of a professed monk. A choice had to be made. Always choices.

If he took his final vows, his clothing would be given to the poor. If he declined vows, or lost his calling on the journey to them, as in the present case, he would change into his old clothes and would leave the monastery immediately.

Later that same day, Servant Jonathan, the abbot, assigned the little monk to go to town and take loaves of freshly baked bread to the poor and the ill.

He hurried off to the monastery bakery so he could enjoy the pleasant scent of bread in the making. He often stood close to the hot bricks of the ovens, warming his crippled body all the way to the bone. He had been hit some time ago by a horse and carriage gone wild. He leaned against the ovens, his hip as warm as bread and his eyes closed in dreams only a monk would understand.

The little monk enjoyed the task of delivering fresh bread to the needy. He loved the feel of the warm bread against his chest as he carried arms full of bread to the village. The odor of the yeast had an earthy, sensual smell to it. The little monk sniffed the air with every step he took. His lungs filled with the deep aroma of the fresh bread. The smell of the bread always sent his thoughts off to communion and those solemn words of Jesus embedded in the liturgy: "This bread is my body broken for you."

He followed his usual round of stops, always ending at Goodie Townsend's little shack.

This day he found her sitting alone and sad. Before he even asked, she blurted out her story. She must take her parents to a place where they could receive constant care. Their bodies were worn out and their minds gone. "Whatever am I going to do?" she asked.

The little monk had no answer for her. He knew that the world is too quick to give shallow answers to life's hardest questions and decisions.

"There are times when we must surrender loved ones into the keeping hand of God," the little monk offered finally. "At the end of our ability, at the foot of the bed, stands the Great Physician," he added with supreme confidence in the One who promises.

Before the little monk left, he wrote a poem for Goodie Townsend—a prayer poem. He had a special gift for writing prayers and poems for those in distress. He usually left them in inconspicuous places, to be found later: by a mincemeat pie, under a lace doily, near a vase of flowers, under a pillow, on a mantle, in a hat or beneath a cup of morning tea.

He left the following poem for Goodie Townsend under a loaf of bread, in her favorite rocking chair beside the fireplace:

> In the worst of decisions, and in their telling,
>   A part of who we are is always diminished.
> Yet, later on, as time covers the moment like dust,
>   We once again learn to trust
> That, in all of this, our hearts have grown,
>   And our fragile spirits made strong and finished.

Goodie had a neighbor who hovered around her porch, scaring off the local children with his skeleton figure and a patch over one eye that hung loosely from its socket. He had been hit in the head with a harpoon and had fallen into the sea on a whaling trip to faraway places years ago.

He kept a close watch on everyone, even the little monk. "Beware of each step you take," said the old man. "Each step you take becomes a path, each path becomes a journey and each journey becomes a destiny."

" 'Beware your journey, little monk,' said the old man..."

This surprised the little monk, for the old man rarely spoke. With his one good eye, the old man glared with such intensity that his eye seemed luminous to the little monk. It seemed to glow with a knowledge of the little monk's soul. "Beware your journey, little monk," said the old man, his back bent from the burdens of life.

The little monk stepped off the porch and hobbled away as quickly as he could.

During his trek across the village green, the little monk saw, at a distance, the monk who had been dismissed from the monastery. Brother Edward sat on a bench, his head bent over, his eyes looking at the ground. No sadder looking man had the little monk ever seen than this man who had given up the high calling of monastic holiness.

But the little monk walked on by. He should not speak to the man. The monastic rule said: Never come to justify or take the side of one being disciplined.

Not speaking, though, was not in the little monk's nature. Yet, there was the mandate of the abbot. Besides, the little monk had come to distribute bread to the poor and infirm. That's my duty today, he thought.

After delivering the rest of the bread, on his way back through the village, he came upon Brother Edward again. The little monk inched up behind him. The man still sat leaning on his elbows, looking at the ground. Such despair, thought the little monk.

Brother Edward turned suddenly, his face filled with a smile.

"You're not brokenhearted at leaving the monastery?" asked the little monk.

"No, no," replied Brother Edward. "On the contrary, I'm not really leaving the monastery behind. I'm taking it with me. Maloo is a moveable feast. I'm taking it to the common folk."

"The man still sat leaning on his elbows."

"But you looked so weighed down," remarked the little monk.

"I was only watching an ancient civilization—an anthill. I'm a keen watcher of ants. I learn so much from them," said Brother Edward. "Their ways are the ways of common folk."

The little monk decided that he, too, would be a keen observer of ants and their ways.

"What did you mean about taking the monastery to the common folk?" asked the little monk.

"Why should the monastery know more about prayer and the devotional life than everyday people? I want the common folk to be monks of the ordinary life, to become 'everyday monks,'" replied Brother Edward. "That's my calling. That's my crusade, my passion, my bliss."

"Then do it with all your might," encouraged the little monk.

"It all came to me night before last when I discovered what it means to pray without ceasing. I remembered my uncle Philip, the kindliest man I know, a man of considerable prominence, but a man of shallow faith. What an everyday monk he would make with but a few insights from the monastery at Maloo."

"I know people like that, too—a lot of people," answered the little monk. "They don't become holy because they never intended to do so."

"It comes down to this," continued the brother. "Evagrius the Solitary, one of the desert fathers said, 'We all have a monk in the heart.'"

Yes, thought the little monk, there is a monk in each of us that craves a life with God, that reaches out to embrace all that the monastery stands for.

"What will you teach the common folk?" the little monk asked.

"I will teach them of silence and solitude, of the glory of the psalms, of mindfulness as a way of life, of the prayer without ceasing, of practicing the presence of Christ and all the other treasures that have been ours," replied Brother Edward.

"So, you're all right, then, with this?" asked the little monk.

"Let's just say that I am at peace," said the brother.

"Then I must leave you and return to the monastery," replied the little monk. Before leaving, the little monk searched his mind for an appropriate scripture verse to bolster the brother in his decision to go and gather an army of everyday monks.

"Let me send you off with this word from Deuteronomy: 'Out of heaven he made you hear his voice to teach you. On earth he showed you his great fire, and you heard his words from out of the fire,'" quoted the little monk.

The little monk turned away slowly and left behind the man of big dreams.

As he walked along, the little monk considered his meeting with the brother. The little monk felt very akin to anyone given a calling to encourage the common folk to nurture the monk who lives in their hearts.

The common people have such capacity for true devotion, he thought. What a world it will be when the least of us becomes a monk in daily life, he concluded. Whenever I can, he decided, I will go out of my way to support these everyday monks.

On his way home to the monastery, the little monk enjoyed the silence and solitude of his journey through the rugged places. The silence was broken only once, by the sound of a shepherd's flute in the distance.

The joy of God so caught him up that even his painful hip could not keep him from dancing a few awkward steps on the dusty road. Then he started to hum some tunes,

finally singing out a song he had written for himself. He
called it "The Little Monk's Song."

Out of the city so hard and gray,
    Into the woods I go in May,
Through enchanted meadow and past the running deer,
    To the land waiting beyond the river.

Refrain:
Yes, I stop. Pray—
    Seven times a day,
    As I gaze on God.
Filling the years, season by season, day by day,
    Giving God my fears, along the rocky road
    and crooked way,
Yes, I stop. Pray—
    Seven times a day,
    As I gaze on God.

Among the lion of the mountain and the birthing goat,
    Into the lone, high places, I long to go,
Until my wearied foot lands on solid rock,
    And by the side of the road my pilgrim's bag I drop.

Now that my frantic, spinning mind has stopped its rush,
    And I linger quietly by the holly bush,
Only then do I see a clearing in the woods,
    Where angels will banquet me with heavenly foods.

I wrap my battered soul in ragged robe,
    And think deep thoughts of God, like Job,
While my wakened heart, freed of its encumbered past,
    Runs childlike into your arms at last.

When the little monk arrived where the flute sound had come from, no one was there. But, by the side of the road, lay a smooth, worn flute. He picked up the flute, put his fingers over the holes and blew a few random notes. The flute almost played itself, as sweet sounds flowed from it effortlessly and in time with the music of the celestial spheres.

5. Mindfulness Is a Habit of the Heart

On one of those special days when butterflies are aware of the wind and bees know the best hiding places of succulent pollen and squirrels can see an acorn yards and yards away, the little monk walked in the garden. He listened for the wisdom of the garden.

The little monk remembered that his mother always referred to such glorious days as "the eighth day of creation."

"Why do you call it that?" he had asked her.

"Well, on the first seven days of creation, all the laws of creation were set in motion, but on the eighth day, the whole of creation hummed away at its fullest," she replied.

Looking out upon this day when the fragrances of the flowers made him drunk and the beauty of the fields made him blind and the sounds of the forest echoed so loudly it made him deaf, the little monk concluded, "This is an eighth day of creation."

Suddenly, though, as he walked along the garden path, he stepped on a daisy, accidentally breaking its stem at ground level and flattening the head of the flower.

He knelt on the ground, picked up the flower and held the broken flower in his hands.

"Why am I so careless and reckless in your world, O God?" he cried out.

He dug a shallow grave and buried the daisy. He looked around to see if anyone saw what he had done. What does one say in memory of a dead daisy? he wondered.

Then he remembered a saying he had recorded long ago in his journal. Easily did the words come back to him, words from the wisdom tradition of the Talmud: "Every blade of grass has its angel that bends over it and whispers, 'Grow, grow.'"

This daisy will never have the chance to grow, to know the full potential God intended it to have, he thought. There will be an empty patch of earth where this flower should have lived out its life. His mother used to say, "Whenever you see a bare patch of earth, that's a reserved spot, the place where a flower should have grown, had it not died before its time. Stop for a moment of silence whenever you see such bare patches spotting the land and offer a prayer."

"I will never forget you, my sister in the universe," said the little monk. "I make you this promise. In paradise I will ask my heavenly Father to allow you to grow again in my eternal garden. In that garden above, I will surround you with love. No foot will ever again tread upon your beauty, nor shatter your simplicity, nor mar your innocence."

The little monk stood there, seized by wonder in the fields of the Lord. A butterfly flew in on the wind and landed on the flower's tiny grave, slowly flapping its rainbow wings in a final good-bye to the daisy. A bee buzzed around, circling the freshly mounded earth. High up in an oak tree a squirrel stood at attention on its hind legs and watched the scene below.

In the moments that followed, the little monk remembered another one of his mother's sayings as she sat on their porch one day, looking out on a bed of flowers: "Save one lily from being crushed and eternity will be yours."

"A butterfly flew in on the wind and landed on the flower's tiny grave..."

The little monk went off to the morning chapter meeting for further instruction in monastic principles and practices.

All the monks sat in silence for a half hour awaiting the arrival of the Inward Teacher, the Holy Spirit.

When Brother Egan sensed the presence of Christ in their midst, he made a small sign of the cross on his forehead, on his lips and on his heart. With a mind fixed on Christ, his lips committed to speaking the truth and his heart surrendered to God, Brother Egan went to the front of the room to offer some instruction.

"What do you know about *The Rule of St. Benedict?*" he asked.

After a brief wait, a few of the monks offered short answers.

"Didn't St. Benedict write it around the sixth century?" one asked.

"I've heard that it is the wisest of the monastic rules and the one most marked by common sense," another responded.

"It's the rule all Benedictine monks and nuns observe today," a third concluded.

"And why call it a *rule?*" asked Brother Egan. No one answered.

"Little monk, do you know?" asked Brother Egan.

But the little monk's mind was on daisies. "I'm sorry. I didn't hear you. A friend of mine died today. I was thinking of that."

"Yes, that's the Rule," said Brother Egan as if the little monk had answered his question. "A *rule* is a collection of bedrock principles by which the community of believers lives. Benedict just happened to have written the best and the wisest of those rules."

Does *The Rule of St. Benedict* cover the death of daisies? wondered the little monk. Later on, he discovered that it did.

"Our topic for discussion today from *The Rule of St. Benedict* is mindfulness," declared Brother Egan. "Mindfulness is that habit of the heart of being fully aware at all times that everything in creation is important to the heavenly Father and therefore to us."

Such a notion struck a good chord, a happy note, within the little monk. He began to listen, rather than just hear. Then he remembered the teaching mentioned earlier from Benedict about the importance of listening. *"Obsculta!"* "Listen!" Benedict had written this as the very first word of the rule. But, it's often the last lesson we ever learn, concluded the little monk.

"Today, you will understand something of the heart of Benedict—his teaching on mindfulness, which is the teaching on possessing and using all things with careful awareness," Brother Egan began.

"Benedict says, 'Nothing is so inconsistent with the life of any Christian as overindulgence.'

"You well know that, as a monk, you own nothing at all. Whatever you need is on loan. This is done so that your only craving, your only desire, will be to possess God and him alone."

The little monk looked at his robe and sandals and the prayer rope around his waist. God owns these, he thought. Then he looked at his Bible and his prayer book. God owns these, too. Then he looked at his hands and feet. These are his, too, he noted. He had nothing and yet he had everything. This was the principle adhered to by all the mystics—the principle of detachment from all things, so that our souls may attach themselves to God alone.

He remembered the story of St. Remegius, a bishop of the medieval church. The bishop's splendid residence caught fire and burned to the ground. In holy detachment,

St. Remegius said, "A fire is a beautiful thing to watch." That's detachment, thought the little monk.

"Now let me tell you the other side of mindfulness. In being mindful of all things, one is held accountable for the use of all things," continued Brother Egan.

"Our Lord himself taught us that God, having created all things, therefore cares for all things, whether it's a lily of the field or a sparrow falling dead from the sky. Even the hairs of our heads are numbered."

Brother Egan noticed that the monks started to lose their concentration. Even the little monk seemed distracted, looking intently at something outside the window. Brother Egan walked to the window to see if he could discover what had captured the little monk's attention, but Brother Egan saw nothing. Yet, he felt sure that the little monk was absorbing a big lesson from some small happening in nature just beyond the monastery window.

Brother Egan turned to a practical example. "Do you know Brother Kelpius?" he asked.

"Isn't he the cellarer for the monastery?" a brother asked in return.

"That's right. He's the cellarer, the custodian, the care-taker of all the monastery's goods. That means that he is responsible for the distribution of food, clothing and tools. Benedict gives these qualifications for a cellarer: He is to be 'someone who is wise, mature in conduct, temperate, not an excessive eater, not proud, excitable, offensive, dilatory or wasteful, but God-fearing and like a father to the whole community.'"

"If only those who were leaders in the world could be so qualified," reacted one of the brothers.

"Especially if one also added the idea of mindfulness in all things," replied Brother Egan. "For you see, Benedict insisted that all utensils and goods of the monastery be regarded as sacred as the holy vessels on the altar, allowing nothing to be neglected or misused or abused."

"Surely you don't mean that rakes and hoes, forks and spoons, wheelbarrows and dinner plates should be treated as if they were the silver chalice and the polished paten used for communion," remarked one of the brothers.

A furrow formed on the brow of Brother Egan. The monks had missed the point of his teaching. "That is exactly what Benedict taught and that is what you will practice as long as you are in this monastery. You are all custodians of whatever is within your reach," Brother Egan declared with a fierceness in his voice.

Brother Egan reached for a shepherd's staff and held it out in front of him. "Anyone who has not learned the lesson of mindfulness will carry this shepherd's staff for the next week, morning, noon and night, whether eating or sleeping or whether praying in the oratory or chanting in the chapel. When this staff has become part of you, and you care for it as you do your own body, then you will have learned the first step in mindfulness. Later on, perhaps, you will know how to walk across the grass without crushing it."

The brother who had missed the point of the lesson started to get up to take responsibility for the shepherd's staff, but the little monk, remembering his careless crushing of the daisy, stepped in front of the other monk and grasped the staff.

"Little monk," said Brother Egan, "you are held accountable for this staff until this time next week. Should you lose it, break it or otherwise mar it, you will be asked to leave the monastery. Is this clear to you? At all times, you will be mindful of the shepherd's staff. This is a promise you make. Do you understand, little monk?" asked Brother Egan.

"I understand," said the little monk, taking the staff and returning to his seat, trying to do so without hitting the heads of the other monks or scraping the backs of chairs.

This won't be easy, thought the little monk.

Brother Egan had one final teaching about mindfulness. "Benedict tells us that the cellarer or caretaker of the monastery 'should not be prone to greed, nor be wasteful and extravagant with the goods of the monastery, but should do everything with moderation.' The true believer never wastes anything. To conserve, preserve, protect, repair, restore and reuse are all appropriate actions of sincere Christians."

"Is there another word for *mindfulness?*" asked one of the brothers.

"*Awareness,*" another brother suddenly shouted with insight.

Brother Egan smiled. "Yes, awareness. Let me tell you a story from the desert fathers," he continued:

"One day a teacher and his disciples went on a long journey in silence. In a note written in the sand, one of the disciples asked the teacher for some special wisdom to meditate on in the silence.

The teacher wrote a word in the sand: 'Awareness.'

'Awareness?' the disciple wrote back in the sand. 'Isn't *awareness* too brief a word for a good meditation? Can you explain what you mean by *awareness?*'

With his finger, the teacher scribbled in the sand, 'Awareness, awareness, awareness.'

'But what does it mean?' the disciple scrawled back quickly in the loose sand.

The teacher stooped down and wrote a new commandment in the sand, 'Be aware.'

'But I don't understand what that means,' wrote the disciple again in the shifting sand.

'Awareness means . . . awareness.' Thus wrote the teacher who had reduced the concept as low as one could go." Brother Egan had finished his story. He watched the monks to see if they got the point of the story. "Look at your buckets. Your wash bucket should be as sacred to you as the communion cup."

"Gorbon Kreeg, a great teacher from the village, says that the commandment to 'be mindful in all things' is the Twelfth Commandment, after the Ten Commandments and the Love Commandment," reported one of the novices who had talked with Gorbon Kreeg at some time or other.

"Gorbon Kreeg is often wise," Brother Egan noted cautiously. "It's time for Noonday Prayer. Let me close with these grand thoughts from *The Rule of St. Benedict:* 'Be mindful of everything; pray without ceasing; eat, drink, and sleep in moderation; love mercy; speak the truth with heart and lips; injure no one; enjoy holy reading; honor all people; be humble; sing psalms daily; make peace always.'"

The group dispersed, leaving the little monk sitting alone, reflecting on the outcome of the day. This morning I had a problem—a crushed daisy, he thought. Now I have another problem, a week-long problem—living day and night with a shepherd's staff! He had given up one problem for a bigger one, he thought. Sweeping aside one problem only makes room for another, if one is not careful, he wisely noted. But what has this to do with mindfulness? he wondered. Then, a flash of insight struck him. Being mindful of small things makes us mindful of all things. Mindfulness is like walking quietly around a sleeping baby, lest you disturb it, he concluded.

He got up from his seat to leave, struggling with the shepherd's staff. In being mindful not to break a window, he knocked over a candlestick instead!

"He had given up one problem for a bigger one…"

This mindfulness stuff is a hard teaching, he noted, tipping the staff in order to get it through the door.

That night, the angel of silence touched the monastery in a special way and the monks of Maloo grew in holiness, even in their sleep.

That week, too, the little monk learned to be mindful.

He had promised to keep the shepherd's staff from all harm. Now, a week later, he handed it back to Brother Egan, who looked over every inch of it for a scratch or dent. Finally, Brother Egan noticed a small gouge in the side of the shepherd's staff. What should I do? wondered Brother Egan. What would Benedict do? Then Brother Egan remembered Benedict's teaching that nothing harsh or burdensome should be placed on the monks. One must set high standards but be long on mercy. In the severe regimen of monastic life, one must be mindful of human frailty. Pettiness has ruined many a monastery. Brother Egan moved his hand to cover the scar on the shepherd's staff. Without mercy, thought Brother Egan, a monastery can easily become a gate to hell.

His eyes met those of the little monk. Nothing needed to be said. Brother Egan only nodded, aware of the veiled truth between himself and a little monk.

6. At Home in the Universe

*T*hrough many special dealings of God, the little monk's heart and life deepened and expanded in remarkable ways. The Potter of Paradise had found a vessel of clay strong enough to hold his truth. The people of the valley took notice of a stirring in the land.

The villagers began to talk about the little monk with growing admiration. They gossiped about him over back fences and in the marketplace. In whispers and hushes they would say:

"He has the simplicity of an unhewn log."

"He's a man who studies clouds. He keeps a journal on them. He knows each cloud by name."

"He's as common as a clay pot."

"He seems to live on hidden manna, on celestial food."

"He whispers in God's ear and God whispers in his."

"He inhales the wind and drinks the dew."

"He's as practical as a plow."

"He's made of good dust."

This growing popularity did not go unnoticed by the abbot, who viewed it with some concern. Nor did it escape the eyes of Gorbon Kreeg, a religious zealot who ran a special school in the village. Gorbon Kreeg envied the innocence and simplicity of the little monk.

One day in the beginning of the Advent season, Servant Jonathan, the abbot, announced, "We will go to the woods today for a retreat."

"Why?" asked one of the monks.

"Because a forest is the playground of angels," answered the abbot. "And because we know you will find the love of God there."

"I don't understand," said another monk.

"You see, most people think they can just take or leave God's other creation, the physical world of plants and animals, of mountains and meadows," Servant Jonathan continued.

"God's other creation is not just a backdrop to humanity, but a brother and sister to us. Until you are connected to all of God's creation, you will not know all of the love of God you should. The apostle John received this command in the Book of Revelation: 'Hurt not the earth, neither the sea, nor the trees.'" The little monk wrote this down in his journal. No deep truth escaped his journal.

The abbot scattered the monks throughout the forest as the wind does seeds. "Each of you will be alone for two days. Find the love of God behind each bush. See his grace in a colony of ants. Look for his hand upon the earth, his footprints in the undergrowth. His fingerprints are on the flowers. Search any grove or glen and you will find God there. Listen to what the forest whispers to you about the kindness and faithfulness of God. God loves equally each and every part of his creation."

The monks went off to be alone with the Alone.

Twilight fell by the time the little monk's feet hit the stepping-stones across the creek. On the other side, he swept his hands across the dew-covered leaves of nearby bushes and washed his face with the fresh dew of evening. How mysterious the dew is, he thought. It drops softly from heaven and appears as quietly and as suddenly as the wind does.

He took out his prayer book and read the Evening Prayer aloud for all creation to hear: "Let my prayer be set forth

"Someone had already claimed this cave."

before you as incense, and the lifting up of my hands as the evening sacrifice."

He found a cave and entered it, planning to make it his abode for the night. Just before he got settled in for the night, he saw a pair of eyes in the darkness of the corner. He peered into the darkness and made out the form of a fox. Someone had already claimed this cave for his own.

The fox came out of the darkness and sat down to watch the little monk, who also kept his eye on the fox. The little monk squinted at the fox in order to center on him and perhaps understand his meaning in the universe. The little monk sat motionless. The fox waited for a long time, cautiously sniffing the air, then picked up a small branch and swung it playfully in his jaws.

By playful instinct, the little monk shook his head as if he too had a branch. The fox moved closer and shook the branch again in a playful tease. Finally the fox and the little monk were nose to nose.

The little monk leaned over and took in his own mouth an end of the branch held by the fox. For one high moment of connectedness, man and fox played tug of war with the branch. Then the fox let go and slowly slipped away. The little monk sat for a long, long time with the branch still in his mouth, marveling at what had just been shared with a passing fox.

The little monk left the cave. The night was dark and damp. He went to the edge of the creek and took one of the large stones. In the field near the creek, the little monk stomped himself a bed in the high grass. As all the rugged prophets before him, the little monk used the large stone for a pillow at night. A fog spilled out over the banks of the creek and spread all the way up the valley.

He awoke late in the night to the sound of an owl hooting. He headed back toward the cave to spend the rest of the night there. He leaned against the cave entrance, remembering some conversation from breakfast that morning.

"How will we know when we have succeeded in praying without ceasing?" one of the monks asked over breakfast.

Brother Stephen, the novice master, heard their conversation and answered, "Theophan the Recluse said that when the prayer without ceasing becomes a permanent part of our daily life, we will have within us a small murmuring stream."

Do I have such a stream? the little monk examined himself and then whispered, "O God, give me not only a murmuring stream, but a raging river flooding its banks."

Now, standing by the open mouth of this dark cave, a verse from Canticles stirred within him: "Until the day break, and the shadows flee away, I will go on my way to the mountain of myrrh and to the hill of frankincense."

He stood in silence under the shadow of the high rock. The fog lifted, revealing star after star, each shining its own silent light.

He took out his journal to record the position of each star that appeared one by one. Open to all of God's creation, he studied the stars also. He knew them all by name and they knew him. The little monk leaned back against the rock, sighed and confessed to the Father of stars.

Sometimes the stars seem distant and detached, as if they hardly know that the earth exists, thought the little monk. Other times, like tonight, the stars seem so close you could reach out and rearrange them as if they were oranges on a blue-black tablecloth.

The universe bestows its gifts upon us as generously as God has sprinkled the Milky Way with stars, the little monk noted to himself. This is a good world, he decided.

He went into the hollow of the cave and curled up on a stone ledge. The long day rolled off his body and sleep came easily, but not before a final prayer, "O God, make me a friend of heaven and earth."

7. Dare to Be Disciplined

*T*he abbey bell, the daily voice of God in the ears of the monks, rang softly, calling the community to Sabbath prayers. It echoed across sleepy sheep grazing slowly in the valley of dying leaves. The first frost had pinched the land.

A visitor, a young man, followed the monks of Maloo down the brick walk as they marched off to Morning Prayer. He entered into the "Te Deum" as best he could and soon found himself at one with the saints of all time, "the glorious company of the apostles, the goodly fellowship of the prophets, the noble army of martyrs," and all the common folk, the everyday monks who faithfully serve the kingdom.

After prayers, the young man asked the little monk about whether one needed to seek the disciplines of prayer, fasting and simplicity, in these modern days.

"No," said the little monk and started to leave.

"But I thought you would say yes," said the young man.

"Very well, then, yes," exclaimed the little monk.

"How can you say both no and yes?" puzzled the young man.

"No, if you have no intention of keeping them and, yes, if you're serious about being a Christian," replied the little monk.

"Tell me of the glory of the disciplines," begged the young man.

"There is no glory. Only the arduous work of prayer. A monk's life consists of endless days of uneventful prayer.

"A visitor, a young man, followed the monks of Maloo down the brick walk…"

What transpires in the fierce work of prayer is too deep for words. The disciplines are not a show of spirituality, but a spanking of the soul."

"Here is a prayer to take with you," the little monk said to the young man. "It's from Hildegard of Bingen." The little monk made a habit of giving prayers to people. "I have no money to give, so I give a greater gold—prayers smoothed down by centuries of use and experience."

> Holy Spirit,
> giving life to all life,
> moving all creatures,
> root of all things,
> wiping out their mistakes,
> healing their wounds,
> you are our true life,
> luminous, wonderful,
> awakening the heart
> from its ancient sleep.

Then the little monk went to a willow tree and cut a switch. He swatted the young man playfully across the seat of the pants and handed the switch to him as a souvenir.

"Be thankful I didn't spank your soul," the little monk said.

"I think you did already," replied the young man, smiling at his newfound wisdom.

"The disciplines are so hard and wearisome," one of the monks at the monastery said to the little monk later.

"Impossible," said another.

"Why do we need them?" asked another.

"Let me tell you a story," said the little monk.

"One day in a long ago time, God sent out a decree that he had repealed the classic spiritual disciplines. A cheer went up from the church and the world. Now there would be nothing but an easy Christianity. How happy the people were. But churches, chapels, cathedrals all closed in no time at all. Religious leaders were no longer needed. Darkness spread over the earth. Crime and violence swelled like blazing forest fires. But no one seemed to care. The time of antichrist had come and evil flourished without resistance. Then, ironically, new cries broke forth from the earth:

'Give me prayer!'

'Give me fasting.'

'Give me meditation.'

'Give me simplicity.'

'Give me the disciplines,' they all cried.

"They had forgotten that out of the disciplines flow the rivers of life. Disciplined prayer is the heartbeat of life and faith," declared the little monk.

"Without the disciplines, you will always be a prodigal son or a wayward daughter," the little monk admonished with a passion that made him tremble.

8. Courage Comes from the Same Place As Fear

*O*ne unusually warm day in November, a teacher went in search of the little monk, finding him flying a kite with some village children.

"It's our teacher," the children cried in awe, for those were days when teachers were respected.

"May I speak with you, little monk?" the teacher asked very seriously.

"After you have helped us fly the kite," the little monk said.

"Well, I'm really not in the mood for play," the teacher responded.

"No one should talk of heavy things until they've felt the lightness of a kite at the end of a string," the little monk noted. "The wind that holds the kite aloft is the same air we breathe."

Cautiously, the teacher joined the group in giving the kite more and more string in its climb toward heaven. Finally they all lay down on the brow of a hill to see the sky better. The little monk tied the kite to his big toe. They watched the movements of the colorful kite against the blue sky.

"Now, what did you want to talk about?" the little monk asked quietly.

"All my life I've had this dream of starting my own school," said the teacher. "But each time the opportunity

"The little monk tied the kite to his big toe."

comes, I get paralyzed with fear and never pursue my dream. How can I get over my fears?" the teacher asked.

Before the little monk could speak, one of the children said, "Tears."

"What?" asked the teacher.

"Tears."

"What does that mean?" he asked.

"My happy tears and my sad tears come from the same place," the child explained.

"So?" queried the teacher.

"Well, I guess courage and fear must come from the same place, too," the child concluded.

The teacher started to say, "That's interesting," but right then the kite jumped high in the air and pulled the little monk's toe and foot straight up as the kite fluttered higher and higher. The children burst into laughter and rolled down the hill, spilling into a giggling pile at the bottom.

"But what should I do, little monk?" asked the teacher.

"I think you should roll down the hill, too," answered the little monk, untangling the string from his big toe.

"Sometimes the answer is found at the very bottom of the hill, not at the peak," said the little monk as he jumped off the bank in order to roll down the hill to the children below.

The teacher started to walk away, but then, with abandon, he leaped off the bank in order to roll down to where wisdom was.

The little monk gave this advice to the teacher who was afraid to start his own school: "Go down to the roaring sea at night and stand in its surf. The sea at night is like a dog that growls and shows his teeth until it knows that you are not afraid of it. Sometimes our big dreams in life come to us as growling dogs. But when you show that you're not afraid of them, they become friends."

The teacher was not used to being taught, especially through kites and children's games and roaring seas and growling dogs. But he soon learned to love these parables of life, especially after the little monk gave him this Bible verse from Hosea: "I have also spoken to the prophets, and I gave numerous visions; and I used parables through the ministry of the prophets."

The little monk gave the kite to the teacher. Later on, the teacher went out on a windy day to fly the kite. "This kite is like my dream," the teacher said. He flew the kite and a month later he flew his dream. He started his own school.

"How bold. How courageous," people said of him.

9. Dealing with Difficult People

A lawyer with a crooked nose once came looking for the little monk, only to find him in the shed sorting seeds.

"Little monk," said the lawyer, "I am weary of obstinate and nasty people. What can I do?"

"What do you want to do?" asked the little monk.

"I want these people not to be so difficult," responded the lawyer.

"They are difficult to you because they inconvenience you. They take your time, your energy, your emotions. But they are most difficult to you because you allow them to be. If your own heart were right and at peace with God, these people would not bother your own peace of mind," said the little monk.

"But isn't it right to get these people to change?" inquired the lawyer.

"Better still to change yourself," replied the little monk. "In trying to change others, you turn yourself into someone you do not like. Trying to change others only drags you down," the little monk offered. "Change yourself and forget changing the world."

"Life shouldn't be like that," the lawyer said.

"You will spoil your own soul if you spend yourself worrying about what life should or shouldn't be," noted the little monk. "Why can't you give up running the universe?"

"The smell of dung stung the lawyer's nose."

"Because people can be so frustrating at times," said the lawyer sadly.

"Let the water flow beneath the bridge," the little monk said. "Let the issue go. Let people go. Don't tie up your own spiritual condition with what other people are doing. If you do, you'll lose your soul, for then you place your soul in the hands of others.

"Brother Fénelon, in his *Spiritual Letters*, taught wisely that you can't change people. Some people will always be weak, vain, fickle, unreliable, unfair, hypocritical and arrogant. The world will always be worldly. You cannot change that, any more than you can change people's personalities. Learn to bear with these people. For his own reasons, God permits people to have their habits or to be unreasonable, irritable or unjust. Do whatever you can, quietly and gently and leave the rest to God."

"What does all this mean for me?" asked the lawyer.

"It means that it is best to let God deal with the faults of others, while he deals with your own faults. In the meantime, learn to tolerate and bear with the imperfections of others. Work on earning your neighbor's love, and their oddities will soon fade into the background. Learn, too, that love is the medicine of heaven for healing human relationships."

At that the lawyer took leave, thinking to himself that the little monk was not as wise as others thought. The little monk really didn't have a very deep understanding of life after all, thought the lawyer. In fact, this little monk is too simple-minded to understand the ways of the world, he concluded.

He watched as the little monk took a few seeds, named each one of them after village children, laid them gently in a bed of chocolate-colored loam and covered them over with a second layer of soil. The little monk added a cup of dung to grow on and sprinkled the whole lot with water from the springs. "People are like seeds. They need a lot of good nurturing," said the little monk.

The smell of dung stung the lawyer's nose. He shook an unbelieving head and left quickly.

That very day, the lawyer went in search of another teacher.

The little monk sang one of his favorite church hymns as he sat in the shed sorting more seeds:

> I sing a song of the saints of God,
>   Patient and brave and true,
> Who toiled and fought and lived and died
>   For the Lord they loved and knew.
> And one was a doctor, and one was a queen,
>   And one was a shepherdess on the green:
> They were all of them saints of God,
>   And I mean, God helping, to be one too.

His mind turned to deeper thoughts about seeds, of how George Fox and the Quakers used the idea of the seed to represent the manifestation of God in the mind. How important, the little monk thought, to have faith in a seed. "Lord, teach me the language of the forest, and to understand the voice of the seeds." Then he remembered that, in school, they had studied about how seeds get dispersed through the forest and beyond.

Some of these seeds, he learned, are blown on the wind, while others bobble along on the surfaces of creeks to new destinations. Some are carried by squirrels to the tops of trees and then fall in hidden places. Some seeds are in pods and, at the ready time, explode all over. Other seeds stick to the backs of bears and are walked to new locations. And others, like pine cones, are picked up by children or animals and moved to new growing places in the sun. Some are carried on branches and twigs by beavers making a new home. The whole creation cooperates in the dispersion of seeds so that every plant can be born again in those seeds so intricately sown throughout the forest.

There must be endless possibilities within these seeds asleep on the forest floor, thought the little monk, awed by the mystery of the seeds. So it is with the seed of the word of God, concluded the little monk.

Just before he left the shed, he noticed something on the edge of the potting bench—a clove of garlic. It had not been there yesterday. It had been placed there so deliberately that he looked for a note, but found none. He picked up the clove of garlic and opened a book on herbs and other plants to read of its purported use in healing. He took it to lunch that day, went to the kitchen and dropped the clove of garlic in the monks' soup, the meager fare for the day.

The novices were tense with each other that day, for they were beginning to see how hard is the life of a monk. Each day wears off a bit more of the world, while the spirit has not yet come fully alive.

But hearty soup is a good tonic for bad moods.

Soon, the little monk heard a praise all cooks love to hear: hungry dinner guests gulping their soup and smacking their lips in delight. "Best soup I ever had," said one of the novices.

The little monk smiled at the power contained in a clove of garlic.

Yet, lest they crave food too much, one of the novices told the story of a monk in another monastery in another time—a monk broken by food. "He conquered everything else in monastic life except his craving for good food," reported the novice. "He finally left the monastery and became a fat chef."

The other novices all looked at him in puzzlement, until he broke out laughing.

Still, they reassured each other how important it is not to be addicted to food.

At the end of the meal, someone brought the usual bowls of soapy water so each monk could wash his own dishes. But one novice took his spoon, dipped a little of the soapy water, slurped it and declared, "Best soup I ever ate." Laughter went down the line of monks.

Even the abbot had to smile.

10. To Whom Should I Give My Money?

"There's a beggar at the gates," a rich man once said to the little monk. "Shall I give to him?"

"Do you want to give to him?" asked the little monk.

"You didn't understand my question," responded the rich man.

"Still, do you want to give to the beggar?"

"Well, I, ah...well, you see...I, ah...well, you never know if they're real beggars or not. They may be just pretending," the rich man said. "You never know...he might squander the money on drink."

"We are commanded to offer charitable gifts. The Holy Spirit, speaking in the Book of Proverbs, said, 'He who is gracious to a poor man lends to the Lord.' Again, the Spirit says in Deuteronomy, 'You shall open your hand wide to your brother, to the poor and to the needy in the land.'"

"Yes, I have been taught that from my youth up," declared the rich man, knowing that he rarely practiced it.

"It is right that we train our hearts in giving alms," said the little monk. "Real saints have always been unable to keep anything for themselves, have always trusted in the one who owns the cattle on a thousand hills, the one who calls us not to be anxious for what we shall eat or wear, but to seek first the kingdom of God."

The little monk spoke this parable:

"Some members of the king's court decided to put together an orchestra to entertain the king. However, they were short of artists. They had more instruments than musicians. Finally one more musician came and they tried to settle on an instrument for him. 'Would you like to play the tuba?' they asked. 'No,' he replied. 'It's too awkward.' 'Would you like to play the drums?' they asked. 'No, they make too much noise,' he answered. 'Would you like to play the saxophone?' they inquired. 'No, that's much too complicated for me,' he responded. 'Well, we have nothing left but this tiny piccolo,' they indicated to the stranger. 'I'll take that,' he announced; 'it's just my size.'

"So the orchestra formed and played for the king. The musicians made music with all their heart and moved the king greatly. He was so moved that he announced that each member of the orchestra could go to the king's treasure house and fill his musical instrument with gold. And there stood the one musician with nothing but his piccolo."

"But what does the parable mean?" asked the rich man.

"Here is the meaning of the parable," said the little monk. "Miserliness robs us of golden opportunities. Miserliness and the kingdom of God are at odds with each other."

"Should I give to anyone who asks?" queried the rich man, pushing his bag of coins farther out of sight within his cloak.

"Give generously, freely, frequently, and—as much as possible—give secretly. But give with discretion. Nowhere are you encouraged to give without discernment. 'Don't throw pearls before swine' says the holy word. The rabbis always taught discretion. Be discerning in your giving. It is written, 'When thou wilt do good, know to whom thou doest it. Give unto the good and help not the sinner.' Another also wrote, 'He that gives a free offering, should give it with a well-meaning eye.'

"No matter how discreet you are, though, there will be times when a person will deceive you. Simply leave the matter there. It's now God's problem. You gave out of the goodness of your heart. If you're deceived by a pretended beggar, one who only spends on his vices, the issue is God's. You have been a faithful steward."

The rich man grew nervous with the direction of this teaching. He hoped to avoid giving any coins at all to the beggar at the gate. There was much the rich man could do for himself with that money.

"But doesn't it look bad to have these beggars around?" asked the rich man. "Shouldn't they be outlawed and their needs handled some other way? Shouldn't there be some kind of community fund to help them?"

"Perhaps, but until then they do serve as a continuous visual sermon, a parable against greed," replied the little monk.

The rich man went speechless.

As the rich man tried to exit, the little monk asked him to repeat this prayer with him:

> O Lord,
> Teach us compassion.
> Let our hearts go out to those in your kingdom
>   who must beg their daily bread.
> May our lengthy prayers never excuse us from
>   paying the price of compassion.
> May our praying never be a substitute for giving.
> Remind us that we are all beggars of some sort
>   in the kingdom of God.

The rich villager went away sorrowful. With drooped head and cloak pulled tightly around him, he walked quickly by the blind beggar at the gate who sat with hands

"He walked quickly by the blind beggar."

cupped in front of him to receive whatever the day might bring of castaway coins.

Later, a waif came up to the little monk. "A man said to give you this," reported the child, holding out a stone.

"What man?" asked the little monk.

The child turned to point to the man, but the man had disappeared into the swarming crowd of the marketplace.

"Was he a rich man?" the little monk asked.

"No, not rich. More like a shepherd."

The little monk scratched his head, then took the stone and rolled it over and over in his hand. Specks of jade glinted in the sunlight. He smelled the stone and knew that it came from near the river.

He placed the stone in the hand of the child who went away joyful.

11. When a Mother Dies

*C*hristmas is always hard on those who grieve for a lost one.

This was the first Christmas that the little monk spent alone without his mother.

Before the final journey to Maloo, while still in Rome, the little monk had received a message encouraging him to return home—his mother was very ill.

By the time he got home, a month later, she had entered her final days.

Even in her illness, she still sang hymns throughout the day. She had a special fondness for the hymn with the words, "In the rustling grass, I hear him pass."

He sat with her for long, slow hours each day. They talked of things small and big. He often smiled at his mother's comments. She saw God in all the details of life. She saw God everywhere. To her, everything became a symbol of the divine. Proverbs spilled from her lips as easily as hello and good-bye came from others:

"If you see two rabbits dancing at the same time," she would say, "that means that God is nearby."

"If you hear the owl call your name that means you will become a saint."

"If you hear water gurgle in a stream, it's really the murmur of an angel."

"If someone has deep brown eyes, you can see eternity in their eyes."

"If you find a door standing open, that means that God is going to bring an opportunity your way."

"If a particular stone catches your eye, you should save it as a reminder that the boy Jesus once collected stones to take to heaven with him as souvenirs."

His mother's bent toward the spiritual in all things fascinated him. "I'll never be able to see the world like that," he said.

His mother died on one of those halfhearted days, a mixture of rain, sleet and snow. Aching cold drove everyone indoors to the warmest stove or fireplace. Except for the whipping of the winter wind, it stayed quiet throughout the day.

The little monk sat in a chair in his mother's bedroom, partly reading, partly listening to her deep breathing, partly surveying the room. He traced faded patterns on the wallpaper stained by the coal smoke. He saw the mouse hole where his mother, with a stiff broom, had shoved visiting mice back through the tiny doorway in the wall.

His mother often spoke to him about the kingdom of the mice who live and labor within the walls of a house.

"They have goals and dreams, justice and mercy, fear and love just like we do," she told him.

Paraphrasing scripture, she remarked, "Go to the mice thou sluggard. Learn from them. They live on scraps and crumbs, yet I say to you, even among those who sit at a king's banquet table, none have more abundance, nor greater gratitude, than the mouse who eats the crumbs beneath our table."

In a vase over by the north window, the little monk saw a bouquet of the last roses of summer. He went over and took the least wilted and faded of them. He brought it to his mother.

"Mother, I have a rose for you. You love roses."

She murmured something, smiled and opened her hand to receive the rose.

"Watch out for the thorns, Mother," he said.

Her hand lay open on the bed and the little monk placed the rose across her hand.

She motioned for him to lean down so she could say something to him. "Remember this promise," she said. "Every Christmas I will dance with you in Moon Meadow."

"What do you mean, Mother?" he asked her. He knew nothing of Moon Meadow. But those were her last words. She slipped into a deep sleep.

The little monk rested his head on the side of the bed. He prayed. He meditated. He sorted memories and weighed each one. Weary from this long vigil, he could watch and wait no more. He fell asleep, but only for a few minutes. Suddenly he was awakened by the unmistakable gurgle of death in his mother's throat. By the time he opened his eyes, she was no more. Now she belonged to the ages.

He noticed that she clenched the rose in her closed fist. Blood trickled from the places where the thorns pierced her skin.

He wiped the blood away, kissed her cheek and said, "Take this rose to Jesus." He touched her ear lobe. It was still warm and soft as the day she was born. The next day he buried her—and the rose.

Now, much later, he was at Maloo, and, as Christmas lay ahead, grief came to haunt him.

The abbot noticed the growing grief in the little monk and talked with him about it. "We sorrow not as those who have no hope," said Servant Jonathan.

"I've been trying to put into words how I feel, so I can talk to God about it," said the little monk.

"When a mother dies," noted the abbot, "it's like a church burning down."

"Yes," affirmed the little monk.

He busied himself carving some animals as Christmas presents for the children of the poor. He gathered hickory branches from the forest and whittled away at his grief.

One evening when the pangs of loneliness came again with memories of home and mother, the little monk sat staring at a lamb he had just finished carving. "Be a lamb even in the midst of hungry wolves," he remembered his mother saying one time at dinner when they were discussing how mean and cruel some people can be.

The abbot's voice broke into the little monk's grieving. "Have you been out tonight?" asked the abbot. "The moon on the meadow is always beautiful this time of year."

The little monk shook himself back to reality. The abbot's words reminded him of his mother's promise: "Every Christmas I will dance with you in Moon Meadow."

"May I go to the meadow?" the little monk asked the abbot.

"Yes" said the abbot, swinging his arm in a wide arc, like a gate opening. "Go, by all means."

Near midnight the little monk arrived at the meadow.

He looked at the moon, trying to take in its meaning. His mother had often said, "If there's a Christmas moon, you can see a manger scene on it. Look hard at it and, with enough faith, you'll see it."

"But how will I know that it's a Christmas moon?" he had asked her.

"When the moon looks seven times larger than at any other time, even a harvest moon, that's a Christmas moon. When it looks so near to you that you could reach out and touch it and stir its surface into puffs of moon powder, then that's a Christmas moon. Rabbits love a Christmas moon. Look for rabbits," she told him.

He did look hard, but saw nothing.

"Two rabbits were at play in the winter snow…"

He waited far into the night for his mother to come dance with him in Moon Meadow.

She's not going to come, he thought. Sadly, he trudged through the snow and ice that covered the meadow. He decided to return to the monastery. The meadow was empty. It seemed that even the animals had gone home for Christmas. A winter silence held fast the frozen tundra of the meadow.

Then, he thought he saw something move in a grove of trees.

Suddenly there came a childlike peeping sound from behind the trees. The little monk turned aside from the path to see what or who was there. In the moonlight two rabbits were at play in the winter snow at dawn. They circled each other, then turned on one foot to circle back the other way. They would jump at each other, retreat, then spin around. They danced before the Lord in the meadow under the moon.

For a time, the little monk swayed, turned this way and that, and shuffled his feet with the rhythm of the rabbits.

Then he plodded off slowly to the monastery. He climbed into bed and pulled the wool blanket over his head to shut out the growing dawn from opening his eyes too wide to the day. In this woolen tomb he fell asleep quickly. The dreams came fast.

"Dreams are parchments from the past, letters from God, messages from our memories," the little monk's mother had often told him.

That early morning he dreamed a strange dream: dancing all night with playful rabbits in the frozen meadow under a cold-steel Christmas moon.

When he awoke later that morning, he turned immediately to thoughts of his mother and of dancing rabbits.

Mothers keep promises, he thought to himself, remembering his mother's dying words: "Every Christmas I will dance with you in Moon Meadow. Look for rabbits. Rabbits love a Christmas moon."

Not only had he seen rabbits. He had danced with them—and his mother—in Moon Meadow.

He wondered to himself, do most mothers keep their promises like this?

12. The First Christmas at Maloo

Winter exploded its fury on undeserving Maloo. Fierce black clouds marched up the valley, crushing out any possible light. Winter war raged outside as frozen wind shook the trees. Ice crystals slashed at anything in sight and snow spewed its insides out all over the land.

Winter had arrived and the little monk was ready to spend his first Christmas at Maloo.

With his cat, Purr, snuggled beside him and a new candle sputtering at the darkness, the little monk wrote the following Christmas thoughts in his journal:

Christmas is in the heart, not under the tree.
You may be the only candle in other people's darkness.
Peace is a prayer on the lips and a cat in the lap.

Purr crept close to the fireplace and stared into the blazing fire, thinking cat thoughts. Silhouetted against the fire, she looked like a contented Buddha. A sudden sheet of cold slid under the door, flickered the candle and nipped at anything warm, whether paws or toes. The little monk held his blue fingers over the candle wick for warmth, then rubbed his toes, while Purr folded her paws beneath her.

Again, the little monk dipped his pen in the blackest of India inks. How many wise thoughts are held in one bottle of ink, he mused, as pen touched parchment and wisdom flowed:

> There are many angels available to minister to us, but none more needed than the Angel Who Oversees Big Mistakes; one of its wings is honesty, the other is sincerity, and when those wings are spread to fly, there is healing in its wings.

Purr jumped to the window ledge to watch snowflakes fall like feathers piling up. The little monk leaned back in his chair and took a long winter's nap. When he awoke, Purr was fast asleep on the window sill. He walked over to look out. A verse of scripture came to mind: "Your sins will be as white as snow." The winter wind whistled a lullaby around Purr's head. The little monk returned to his table and picked up the pen again:

> Silent Night. Silence is the beginning and ending of every spiritual journey, for God dwells in silence. Where are the angels of Christmas First? Not on your tree but in your prayer closet. Where are the wise men of Christmas First? Whispering in your ear, if you will be still and listen like a deer in the forest. Where are the shepherds of Christmas First? Shepherding the celestial flock, who graze among the stars—waiting for you. Where is the Messiah of Christmas First? Just a prayer away!

> Christmas is a time to center down into that still point deep within where we can gaze on God for one small Christmas moment. Then we should go forth like roaring lions, making our presence known in a world that has forgotten the shout of Christian triumph.

Then he wrote a letter to a wayward relative, but soon discarded it, for it seemed too harsh. The monks observed closely the principle: "Every letter you write should edify and build up the soul of the recipient." He began again and finished a letter that would please St. Benedict.

Though the land looked bleak and the stone floor of the monastery had a glaze of ice on it, the little monk's heart burned as brightly as old kindling wood.

Later his mind turned to poetry. Every Christmas since he was nine years old, he wrote a Christmas poem. This year would be no different, as the words of a new poem flowed easily from a pen now loaded full with ink again:

Under the Calvary Tree,
I found your gifts for me.
This night of candlelight and distant bell so low,
This eve of burning logs and deep quiet snow.
Your gifts were wrapped in crimson and blue,
And tied with evergreen and rainbow ribbon, too.
Childlike, I tore the wrappings off—that's what
gifts are for.
Love, wonder, peace—all spilled across my life
then and evermore.

Under the Calvary Tree
I found no gift for thee.
Strangers rarely get a gift by name,
They merely sit and smile and watch.
Such an empty game.
Looking 'round, I had nothing of worth to give.
"It takes all I have and more," said I,
"just to live."
Hastily, I wrapped a useless gift, on sudden whim,
Then, weeping, ashamed, tossed that gift aside,
and gave myself to him.

A quiet tap at the door shook the little monk from his contemplative mood. "It's time," said a monk from beyond the door, after offering the customary prayer before knocking. The little monk seemed puzzled at first, then remembered that the whole monastery had been invited to a boar's head festival, held at the village church. *"Deo Gratias,"* said the little monk in keeping with the teaching of *The Rule of St. Benedict:* "If a knock comes to the door, the monk is to answer 'Thanks be to God.'"

"Remember," said Servant Jonathan, "each of you may have one small bowl of plum pudding at the end of the festival."

"I've never been to a boar's head festival before," the little monk whispered to one of the other brothers.

The monks lined up down the length of the hallway of the monastery. They would march two by two, carrying torches.

Their hot torches melted the falling snow, changing the snow into droplets of rain. The festival always began when the marching monks came into sight over the brow of the hill. They came chanting one of the "O" antiphons of Christmas, "O Key of David, and Scepter of the house of Israel, you who open and none can shut, who shut and none can open," as they tromped along through the snow. Bells rang, children cheered and dogs barked when the monks came into view. Then everything went silent as snow.

A good boar's head festival always started with this reverent quiet as the torches were blown out. Everyone entered the hall. All light was extinguished. A hush fell over everyone there.

From a corner of the room an orchestra struck up a song of worship. Then came the heavy, rhythmic stomp of the king's beefeaters, sounding like history marching in. A tiny sprite broke the darkness, carrying in a lighted taper. The sprite moved to the altar where she passed the light to the priest who, in turn, lit the great candle in honor of Christ, Light of the World.

The little monk held his breath as candles of all sorts throughout the church flashed their warm invitations. The townspeople carried in the Yule log, as everyone sang, "Deck the halls with boughs of holly." They decked out the whole church with holly, ivy, candles and festive trim of golds, royal blues and stripes of purple and orange.

The church came alive with the sound of joyful music:

> The holly and the ivy
>   When they are both full grown
> Of all the trees that are in the wood
>   The holly bears the crown.

The words of the plaintive song sank deep in the little monk's heart:

> The holly bears a blossom
>   As white as the lily flow'r....
>
> The holly bears a berry
>   As red as any blood....
>
> The holly bears a prickle
>   As sharp as any thorn....
>
> The holly bears a bark
>   As bitter as any gall....

Then from the back of the church came waifs heralding the generosity of Christmas, when gifts are given and promises kept. Gaily did they sing:

Here we come a-wassailing, Among the leaves so
green.
Here we come a-wassailing, So fair to be seen.
We are not daily beggars. That beg from door to door,
But we are neighbors' children, Whom you have
seen before.

More singing followed. The little monk's eyes danced
with the beat of each new note. Caught up in all of this, the
little monk was not prepared for what quickly followed.
Doors banged open with a crash. Children screamed, and
the little monk ducked his head down in his robe like a
turtle. Trumpets blared as knights came in bearing the
boar's head, a plum pudding and a mince pie.

"What's that?" the little monk asked another, less frightened monk.

"That's the boar's head on a platter. The boar's head is
the symbol of evil. The boar has been defeated in the triumph of Christ. The plum pudding and the mince pie sig-
nify that through the victory of Christ over evil, God is able
to bestow all kinds of good and gracious gifts upon us."

The little monk understood all too well now the amazing
grace of God.

The traditional Christmas story and manger scene followed, reminding everyone that Christ came into the world
through the best door available for such a grand entrance—
a woman's womb. Now, the sharing of food began. When
the last bite of plum pudding had been licked from the
bowl, the monks lighted their torches again for the march
back to the monastery.

As they went out the door, one of the monks motioned
that the little monk still had plum pudding on the side of
his mouth. Along with a brief prayer of gratitude to God for

such a joyous time, the little monk licked the remaining plum pudding from the side of his mouth.

When they got outside the church, though, the snow had turned into a fierce storm. They had to lean into the wind in order to push ahead. Huge gusts of wind and snow soon snuffed out the torches. The monks tried to hold onto the robe of the monk in front of them. But the little monk fell behind because of his limp. Within minutes he was lost from the rest of the group. It did no good to shout, for the wind roared too loudly.

He stood still for a moment in belly-deep snow and tried to listen for some sign of life. But the winter storm was unforgiving. He lost his sense of direction in the heavy snow. He tried to judge as best he could the direction he ought to go. Only one word pounded in his head—lost!

He pulled his body through the snow like someone trying to escape from quicksand. The more he pulled, the farther he sank in the snow. Then he squinted his eyes to pierce the blinding snow and saw something that looked familiar not far in front of him. Three trees. Prophets' Point. He dragged himself to the trees and crawled under the limbs of the holly for shelter. Before falling into an exhausted sleep, the little monk tied his prayer rope on one of the limbs of the holly tree. If anyone comes looking for me, they have a better chance of finding me here beneath the trees of Prophets' Point than anywhere else.

He dreamed a strange dream. A figure, a faceless monk, took a smooth stone and put it in a leather sling to whip it at an eagle. The faceless monk's spinning stone broke the bird's feathered wing. The eagle flip-flopped through the air before crashing headfirst into a cliff. Then the faceless monk arrived at heaven's door, seeking entrance. St. Peter said, "Who have you brought with you?" "I don't know what you mean," said the faceless monk. "I'm here by myself." "But you don't

"He crawled under the limbs of the holly for shelter..."

understand; no one gets into heaven alone," said St. Peter. "Everyone on earth is responsible for someone or something else. The plan was for you to bring an eagle with you. You were responsible for an eagle."

"I didn't know," said the faceless monk. "I killed the eagle." At that, hell coughed up fire and smoke.

The dream agitated the little monk as he tossed and turned, trying to see who the faceless monk might be.

Meanwhile, the other monks had arrived at the monastery and realized that one of their company was missing. It did not take long to conclude that it was the little monk. "This is very serious," said the abbot. "But, there's nothing we can do until the storm lets up. We will wait—and pray." No one slept that night. They all gathered in the refectory to drink hot tea, to nibble a wheel of cheese, to encourage each other and pray for a miracle. The night crept along, even as the winter storm rushed by the frozen windows. Little by little, all talk stopped as each monk fell into a dreamy state, half-awake, half-dozing.

Suddenly, a kicking and banging at the door brought the monastery to life.

When the porter opened the door, a heavy hulk of a man stood there, holding the little monk in his arms. The porter took the little monk in his own arms, but before he could invite the man in, the man had already gone back into the snow, which hid all things.

Half-dead and delirious, the little monk mumbled something about an eagle and a sling. Before passing out again, the little monk said a puzzling thing, "I am that monk," the dream still haunting him.

The porter stood there as the rest of the monks gathered around. "Who brought him here?" the abbot asked, having seen only the outline of a figure disappearing into the snow.

"A shepherd," said the porter looking down at the limp body of the little monk.

13. The Seventh Gift

*O*n the Christian calendar, Epiphany had ended and the days were leaning toward Lent.

The little monk continued to make good recovery. Even Purr had been quite concerned. She never left his side and whenever the little monk awakened, Purr sat looking at him with a nurse's eyes.

The abbot had gathered the whole monastery into the common room in order to offer thanksgiving to God for sparing the life of the little monk and renewing his health.

They shared ginger cookies and cups of boiled coffee mixed with steaming hot milk. And for the little monk, something extra—monks' soup, a terrible concoction of herbs, potatoes and numerous kinds of bitter seeds. One of the monks teased him that some of this same mix of monks' soup had cured many a sick horse in the area.

"Tell us a story," the monks begged the abbot. Servant Jonathan had a reputation for his good stories.

"Here's a story an old shepherd once told me," he said, standing before the large fireplace and telling them a story they never forgot.

"Once upon a time in a faraway land, across the wide meadow and beyond the deep river, there was a happy kingdom. Happy, except for one thing: the princess who was the heir to the throne was spoiled rotten. She was nasty to the servants, refused to make her bed in the morning and never, never would eat her peas or broccoli.

"The king had no sons and only the one daughter. He was growing old and worried about what would happen to the kingdom if he should die suddenly. So he published a mandate that his daughter could not become queen until she had received, in her nature, the seven gifts. 'What are the seven gifts?' she asked her father. 'You will know them when you see them,' he answered mysteriously.

"'You must find them all. Not until you have received the seventh gift will you be given the kingdom,' her father stated.

"'My brother, your uncle, Prince Escobar, will rule until you're ready. By the end of the twelfth month after my passing, you must have found the seventh gift or Escobar will reign for life.'

"Little did the king know that such a plan only set Escobar's heart on fire with ambition and greed. While on the outside Escobar acted pleased for the princess, in his seething heart he swore that the princess would never find the seventh gift nor inherit the kingdom.

"In private, the king said to his daughter, 'Promise me that when I die, you will visit my grave each day for a year.' Reluctant even to consider her father's death, still she said, 'I promise, Father.'

"One night the king died rather suddenly. Escobar took over the kingdom until the princess could receive the seventh gift. But as young people are wont to do, she procrastinated and the months slipped by quickly. She spent much time entertaining her friends in frivolous things. By now, it was nearing the end of the twelfth month.

"Finally, she sent out a message by horse and rider that all in the land were to bring her gifts that she might discover, for the sake of the kingdom, the seven gifts that would make her queen.

"Several days later, thousands showed up at the castle door. They marched across the moat where dragons raised their heads from the scummy waters and spit fire at them. With fear and trembling, the visitors from afar ascended the stone staircase that led to the king's reception chamber.

"'It will take seven days to view all the gifts,' the lady-in-waiting told the princess.

"On the first day the princess saw gold and silver, jewels and fine clothes. But by the end of the day she had a big headache from the various sweaty, pushy hucksters of endless trinkets and treasures—all pressing in on her, wishing for her attention.

"This can't be the kind of gift my father had in mind, thought the princess. 'Give me solitude,' the princess shouted at last. One by one, the disgruntled people dispersed and left her alone. She had never before appreciated such solitude. She heard a whisper within her heart: 'The first gift is solitude.' She looked around quickly for the source of the voice, but no one was there.

"The next day the musicians came to present her with the gift of music. All day the horns blared, the strings hummed, the drums beat furiously. Bands played on endlessly. Finally, the princess cried aloud, 'Give me silence!' and covered her ears with her hands. The music stopped, the marching stopped, the singing stopped. Nothing could be heard but the princess's own breathing and the sound of her own heart beating. She loved how the silence made her feel. In the silence, she heard a soundless whisper: 'This is the second gift.'

"On the third day, she was hounded by the frustration of choosing among so many good gifts. The stress and worry of choosing rightly got to her. She fell into deep weeping and longed for peace. 'Give me serenity,' she wept softly, and the third gift, the peace that passes all understanding, flowed into her. Her heart told her that this was the third gift.

"The princess cried aloud, 'Give me silence!'"

"She treasured these moments of serenity. She vowed never to make a decision again until she had centered herself down into the still point, that hidden place of serenity in all of us.

"On the fourth day, the princess noticed that because of the press of the crowd, many things in the castle were getting broken and that the servants had gathered up the broken tables, chipped china, torn wall decorations and ruined carpets. Something struck her conscience. She remembered a teaching of her father. One time during a banquet a guest leaned back too far in a chair and its legs snapped. She overheard her father whisper to the servant to take the chair to his room.

"Later that night when she went to his room to kiss him good night, she found him repairing the broken chair. 'Father, what are you doing?' she asked. 'Be mindful of everything in creation. Be a friend to the least of all created things. Treat every last thing in the castle as if it were a chalice from the Lord's table,' he advised. Now she knew what her father meant. She began to teach herself and her servants to be mindful of all things. She was grateful to her father now for this fourth gift.

"The princess reserved the fifth day for all the religious leaders in the kingdom to suggest their gifts. But rather than listen to them one by one as they offered a myriad of spiritual gifts, she said to them, 'Meet as a group and tell me the one gift most needful to be a true leader in the kingdom of God.' They looked at each other. They were puzzled by the request. They were in the habit of scorning each other's religion. They certainly would never have thought of meeting together. But, the queen-to-be had spoken. With great fear and suspicion they began to talk to each other. They talked and talked. Through lunch. Through tea time. Through dinner.

"Tension turned to laughter, frowns turned to smiles. Name calling turned to back slapping. Finally, a representative came with their decision. 'To be a true seeker of the ancient secrets, there is one thing needful—to commune with those with whom you differ. It would behoove any great leader to listen to the ideas of all—even those with whom you might disagree. This is a great gift.' The princess knew she would need this fifth gift more than all the others in ruling the kingdom.

"The sixth day came. Most of the people had lost interest by now. But, one unlearned, devout woman stayed behind. She seemed lost in prayer. Her lips moved quietly as if telling secrets to a friend. Her countenance glowed with light from heaven. The princess waited for a long time before the woman opened her eyes. The woman looked around her sadly as if disappointed that she was still on earth and not in heaven. 'What were you doing?' asked the princess. 'Just gazing on God,' came the reply. That was a gift the princess wanted with all her heart. 'What must I do to obtain this gift?' the princess asked. The old woman looked the princess up and down before offering the pearl of great price. 'To gaze on God, you must do three things: eat your peas and broccoli, make your bed in the mornings and behave yourself—don't be a brat,' said the woman bravely.

'Is that it?' asked the princess, expecting all kinds of difficult disciplines to do, rigid practices to observe every day or to be sent into the desert to be a lifelong hermit.

'The commandments of God are not burdensome. His yoke is easy and his burden light,' informed the old woman. That was the day the princess learned to love peas and broccoli and the gaze of God.

"On the seventh day no one had come to the king's chamber yet except the king's fool, the court jester.

"There were no more gifts to be offered. Suddenly, the words of her father echoed in the princess's ear: 'Not until you have received the seventh gift can you become the queen and rule my people.'

"The princess realized, though, that even if she didn't become the queen, her life still would be a gracious one because of the six great gifts already hers.

"Yes, she could be satisfied not to be a queen. She smiled the smile that only contented mystics know. Yet, she owed it to her father and to the people to try to find the seventh gift. But she had nowhere else to look for the last, the seventh gift.

"She was ready to leave the chamber and accept whatever life offered her, when the king's fool somersaulted in front of her, made a crazy face and said, 'You haven't asked for my gift!'

"Surprised, the princess asked, 'What gift could you offer me?'

"'To be a fool like myself,' he said as he stood on his head. 'When you can see life upside down and through a fool's eyes, you will have the greatest gift any leader can have.'

"The king's fool threw confetti in the air, blew on a child's horn and signed the princess's forehead with the sign of a fool—a fool's face, upside down.

"The chamber echoed and echoed with his laughter. Then Escobar entered the chamber and, in counsel with his best advisors, decided that readiness to become a fool for the kingdom was not validly the seventh gift. Before the fool withdrew into the shadows to escape the mockery of the nobles, he leaned over to remind the princess that this was the day she needed to visit her father's grave for the last time.

"When she returned from the graveside later in the day, the crowd hushed. The kingdom is mine, Escobar hissed within himself. To the assembled court, he announced: 'The princess has not found the seventh gift. She will not be the queen. I inherit the kingdom.' Then, mustering all his frustrated authority, he ordered the princess, 'Go to your room.'

"She looked for some encouragement or support among the nobles. They all feared Escobar and turned their eyes to the ground.

"Then, the fool stepped out of the shadows and announced that the princess, after all, had indeed received the seventh gift. The nobles gasped at such boldness before the new king.

"'What do you mean?' demanded Escobar.

"'The princess has received the gift of keeping promises. She promised her father that she would visit his grave every day for a year. She has kept that promise. Today is a year from the day he died. Therefore, she has received the seventh gift.'

"There could be no doubt about the authenticity of the gift. Keeping promises is very important. All the princes and nobles cheered. Escobar started to protest, but then realized he had lost the kingdom. The nobles applauded, the kingdom shook, and Escobar fled the land in a fury. He went into exile in a far country but vowed to return someday to do battle again for the right to the kingdom.

"The princess put on her crown—but upside down. Some of the nobles looked on in amazement. Others snickered a little, but then it dawned on them that she had done it on purpose. They had a fool for a queen and they loved every minute of it. Laughter filled the land and purified the air.

"And so, this queen of the seventh gift ruled her kingdom as if it were the kingdom of God."

Servant Jonathan's story had many lessons to teach. He invited the monks to have more coffee and ginger cookies as they turned to discussing the story. The little monk took his ginger cookie, broke off a small piece for Purr who loved ginger cookies, and nibbled on the rest himself as he thought about the story. In his own heart, he prayed, O God, give me the seven gifts that will make me a good monk.

14. Deep Listening in a Shallow World

*O*ne day in the middle of winter, the little monk sat by the icy river, seeking its secrets of wisdom.

Along came a passerby intent on spending the time by chattering about everything under the sun. The little monk hushed him to silence. "Listen to the river." Each time the man tried to speak, the little monk whispered, "Listen to the river." An hour went by. Finally, the little monk said, "We need more deep listeners in this shallow world of ours."

"I have always tried to be a good listener," said the stranger. "I'm not always successful. But I try."

"So do I," said the little monk. He remembered a river ferryman he once encountered long ago.

"Listen to the river," said the ferryman.

"What will it say?" asked the little monk.

"That's between your soul and the soul of the river. The river has many truths to tell. It shares only what you need for the moment. But the river is a reluctant counselor. It has to be certain that you're ready for its truth. Only the patient will learn the river's secrets."

"What lesson have you learned from the river?" the little monk asked the ferryman.

"I've learned that to be a river is to will one thing. The river never gives up its search for the sea. Nothing stops the river's eternal pursuit of the waiting sea."

"The little monk leaned over the side of the boat…"

The ferryman seemed to be taken into the mystery of the river. "Listen," he said quietly. "What do you hear?" he asked the little monk.

"I hear crickets," replied the little monk.

"What else do you hear?"

"A bullfrog," answered the little monk.

"Listen deeper. Now what do you hear?" asked the ferryman.

"I hear tiny waves beating against the shore," answered the little monk.

"When from deep within you still hear the river lapping at the shoreline of your heart, then will you be ready to hear the still small voice of the Spirit," said the ferryman.

The little monk listened so hard his ears began to ache.

"Dangle your fingers in the river," the ferryman told him.

The little monk leaned over the side of the boat and dragged his fingers in the water.

"When you dangle your fingers in the river," said the ferryman, "you drag a whole universe behind you."

The little monk caught his breath at such a thought. The universe on my fingertips, he mused to himself.

The little monk shared this story of the river and the ferryman with the stranger who had just joined him by the river that flows near Maloo.

"Let me tell you a parable about one of the lost secrets of Nineveh. The parable goes like this," said the little monk.

"The world knew the king of Nineveh as the boy-king. He assumed the throne at age eleven, still young and innocent. Because of his childlike innocence as well as the purity and sincerity of his rule, his kingdom flourished. The people lived in peace and serenity. As the years rolled by and the king matured, he came to be known as 'The King

Who Listens.' His kingdom overshadowed all the king-doms around.

"But as the next several years wore on, the king became preoccupied with kingdom work. The busier he got, the less he listened; the less he listened, the more the quality of living declined and deteriorated. Plagues rampaged the land, the flowers died, animals fled the barren forests, and the people went to war with each other. The king's own wife died and his daughter, overtaken by sleeping sickness, fell into a deep coma.

"In a far corner of the kingdom, there lived a young and handsome prince who had known and loved the king's daughter since the prince was a young lad. He set off one day to see if there might be some magic healing for her. As the prince traveled along on his journey to the castle of the king, it began to pour down rain. He sought shelter in a cave with deep, dark passageways. Lighting a torch, he explored the cave and finally came to a mysterious room. Over the door to the room, carved into the stone, were these words: 'Lost Secrets.'

"Inside a smaller room, he discovered a statue with this inscription at the base: *The Listener.* The statue had a figure, half human and half divine, with one hand cupped to the ear—the symbol of listening. He also found a large casket of treasures with silver, gold, jewels and precious gems. On top of these riches lay an ancient scroll. Unrolling the scroll, he read these words at the top: 'The Five Laws of Listening.'"

"What are the five laws of listening?" asked the visitor.

"Here are the five laws just as they were written on the scroll:

> *Listen to the heart of the other person.*
> *Listen between the lines.*

Listen to what is not said.
Listen with the eyes.
Listen to the silence."

"These are very intriguing principles. Can you explain these things?" asked the stranger as he pulled his coat around him to ward off the growing cold.

"I can, but I shouldn't," responded the little monk. "They are not to be understood by being explained, but by being meditated on until these truths yield up their wisdom, like seeds waiting for the ready moment to break open and bring forth life."

They listened to the crunch and pop of the ice moving on the river.

"Epictetus told us long ago that God gave us two ears and one mouth so that we could listen twice as much as we talk.

"When we learn to listen with the third ear, all these other principles become very clear to us."

"What happened in the end of the parable?" inquired the stranger.

"Well, like all good stories, this one had a happy ending. The young prince took his newly found secret to the king and persuaded him once again to practice the great secrets of listening. The plagues ended and the kingdom prospered. The scent of fresh-blooming flowers awakened the princess from her deep sleep. Her wedding to the young prince was one of the most fantastic in Assyrian history."

The stranger started on another topic, but the little monk again hushed him to silence. "Listen to the river," said the little monk. A piece of poetry formed itself in the little monk's mind:

Listen to the river's ceaseless flow,
And feel the wind's capricious blow.

Purr stretched out flat on her stomach and watched a fish move slowly under the ice. She found a small break in the ice and dipped a furry paw in the cold river and the universe knew it.

15. The Limits of Power

Servant Jonathan, the abbot, sent the little monk to help cobble shoes for the poor. He worked with diligence as an apprentice in the cobbler's shed. Before coming to Maloo, one of the monks had been a cobbler, a craftsman in making shoes. His service to others now called for him to work some part of each day doing that which he knew well—making shoes.

The little monk loved the smell of old leather. He liked the feel of the small nails he held in his mouth, taking them out one at a time to drive them into the heel of the shoe. He learned to sew leather and to stain shoes.

"Remember," said the master cobbler, "any shoe you make for the poor may someday be worn by Christ. You never know when the Stranger from Galilee may come knocking at your door in the guise of a poor person. Make every pair of shoes the best shoes in case an angel unawares ever comes looking for a new pair of shoes."

The master cobbler left the little monk alone one day to care for the work of the cobble shop.

A judge stopped by to see if he could buy some shoes. "You folks make the best shoes around," he told the little monk.

"These shoes are for the poor," answered the little monk.

"Don't you know who I am?" asked the judge. "I'm a judge and I have a lot of power. You'd better learn the truth of who is really important around here."

"'Don't you know who I am?' asked the judge."

"Let me share a parable with you about one of the lost secrets of Nineveh," said the little monk.

"The king of Nineveh was noted for his napping. In the midst of some long report on activities within the kingdom, the king's head would drop to his chest and he would nod off. No one knew for sure exactly what to do. Does one awaken a sleeping king? And if so, how does one do it? Do you clear your voice or cough or touch the king's arm? Should one dare touch the king?

"Those giving reports when the king fell asleep never knew if they should continue or not. After all, the king could be insulted either way—if you stopped or if you just went on. But how does one ask a sleeping king about such things?

"What the people did not know was that the king was really not sleeping, but only pretending to do so. What the king discovered early on was that people spoke the truth when kings slept. So, he would pretend to nod off knowing that this would take people off guard so that they felt free to talk, discuss, speak honest opinions and feelings with each other, yes, even gripe and complain.

"That was when the king heard the real truth about his kingdom and about himself. It was then that he got a true view of the citizens of his kingdom. It was then that he found out who were his real friends and enemies. The king could then act on this information, no one being the wiser except the king himself. The truth is what comes to the forefront when kings are sleeping. Better to be a sleeping king and hear the truth than to be a king wide awake and have the people withhold the truth. Learn this secret: the world is a far different world when kings are sleeping than when they're awake."

"What's your point?" asked the judge.

"My point is that the truth is all around us and often where we least expect it," answered the little monk.

"You see, all truth is God's truth, whether in science, scripture or law. But, it takes all of the truth to have the whole truth. A truth, by itself, may not be all of the truth. St. Thomas Aquinas used to tell people to 'look for all the truths.' And we should do that wearing the lens of faith."

"Why are you talking about truth. I'm talking about power," said the judge.

"Power always distorts truth, but truth, on the other hand, limits power," answered the little monk.

The judge did not like this cross-examination by a simple monk and said so. "Just sell me shoes and we'll end the matter there," the judge grouched.

"No. Matters like these are settled in heaven. The judge of heaven will decide who should get shoes, the rich or the poor. As for now, if you want our shoes, you'll have to buy them from the poor," explained the little monk.

The judge left unhappy that he could not control even a little monk. Judicial power does have its limits, he found.

The little monk returned to making the best shoes he could.

These shoes will be for Gilly, the blind girl, he decided.

16. The Zeal of Gorbon Kreeg

*T*he little monk felt unusually empty and penitent on Ash Wednesday, the threshold of Lent. He wondered how God might fill the emptiness he felt that day.

On this slate gray day, the little monk finished Morning Prayer with a sense of need for his soul. He decided to go to the marketplace, to be in touch with the common folk. He always felt better when mingling with ordinary people, everyday saints.

There seemed to be an odd buzz in the marketplace. He came to a group of people gathered around several young men. "What's going on?" he asked one of the bystanders.

"It's the school of Gorbon Kreeg. Some of his students are showing their skills," came the reply.

"Skill in what?" asked the little monk, trying to size up the situation.

"Skill in the spiritual disciplines."

"What do you mean?" the little monk asked further, always interested in new insights into the spiritual disciplines.

"Gorbon Kreeg trains these young men to be religious perfectionists, to raise many of the spiritual disciplines to an art form. He calls these young men God's 'artists of anguish.'"

The little monk stood at the edge of the crowd. Gorbon Kreeg was introducing some of his disciples, seeking crowd approval. One by one, Gorbon Kreeg paraded the artists of anguish before the crowd. One artist was an expert in fasting.

"One artist was an expert in fasting."

Gorbon Kreeg had several strong men carry in a platform on which sat an emaciated young man who now looked old before his time. Bones stuck out all over. His glazed eyes rested in sunken sockets. He moaned pitifully. He was the very epitome of someone wasted by fasting.

"This man has fasted for sixty-two days." People applauded and cheers went up. The fasting master raised a withered arm ever so slightly in response. "Pray for me that I will be able to fast a hundred days," he implored.

They brought forward a second young man. He seemed very healthy and alert, even charming in his manner with the crowd. "This man," announced Gorbon Kreeg, "this man is accomplished in scripture memory. Any question you ask him will be answered with a Bible verse. For the last three years now he has only spoken Bible verses. Go ahead. Test him."

Someone from the crowd raised a hand. "What time is it?"

Without hesitation, the Bible memorizer responded, "It is high time to awake out of sleep, Romans 13:11." A few people applauded. Someone else asked, "What do you think of the age in which we live?" The Bible memorizer rolled his eyes toward heaven, "My soul is wearied because of murderers, Jeremiah 4:31." More applause. Another hand slipped up high in the air. "What is your name?" The Bible memorizer stared into the person's eyes. "My name is Legion, for we are many, Mark 5:9." And so it went for almost an hour, building to a crescendo of applause.

The last disciple of Gorbon Kreeg moved slowly to the center of the crowd. "This wonder among us has achieved ultimate humility," Gorbon Kreeg told them. "He's an expert in being mocked. Go ahead. Spit on him. Call him names. Ridicule him and see what he does." People were reluctant to be rude or cruel, yet the challenge was there.

Finally someone picked up a handful of dirt and threw it over the front of his clothes. "May God richly bless you for keeping me humble," the humble man responded. Someone else put a dog's bone in his mouth. "Thank you, God, for these blessed companions who point the way to humility." Soon the abuse and name calling got out of hand. Not much later, the man had been stripped naked, spit upon, slapped and pinched, but never lost his composure. With each new round of abuse, the man grew more angelic.

"Thank you; that's all for today. Come back next week and we'll have four new masters of the spiritual disciplines for you to look at, including a Lenten specialist," Gorbon Kreeg announced.

"How do you think it's going?" one of Gorbon Kreeg's disciples asked him.

"The village is mine. I can feel it," Gorbon Kreeg replied.

"That will take a miracle—to capture this village. It's guarded well by the holiness of the monastery," the disciple answered. Gorbon Kreeg looked sourly in the direction of the monastery.

Gorbon Kreeg lived by cunning and cleverness. He was an intuitive man, always listening for a slipped word or an unthinking comment in which he might find the seed of a new strategy, something with which to take advantage of others' weaknesses.

"Yes, what we need is a miracle or two," Gorbon Kreeg decided. "We need a miracle man," he said, taking the shoulder of his disciple. "Come, let's go plan a miracle or two," said a very pleased Gorbon Kreeg.

The crowd began to disperse, but the little monk stood where he was, thinking deeply about what he had just seen and heard. Gorbon Kreeg interrupted his thoughts, "Aren't you the little monk of prayer?" The little monk turned around, surprised that Gorbon Kreeg knew him.

"Yes, I'm the little monk," he said, wondering what Gorbon Kreeg wanted.

"Can I talk to you privately?" asked Gorbon Kreeg, pulling the little monk to the side, under a fig tree.

"I would like for you to become part of my group," whispered Gorbon Kreeg. The little monk could barely hear Gorbon's words. "You could easily become my best disciple," continued Gorbon.

"I don't know..." the little monk started to reply.

"Think of the attention and glory you could bring to the monastery. In a short time, hundreds of new novices would come to fill the halls of Maloo's monastery. You could do more for God than any other monk who has come to Maloo."

"But I have no special talent, no unusual gift," noted the little monk.

"Oh, but you do. You're already known as the little monk of prayer. We can build on that. You'll be as famous as St. Francis. The world will come to hear your wisdom. I can make you into a saint. Perhaps even a miracle worker."

A miracle worker, the little monk thought, teased by the possibility. But something about all this soon made the little monk uneasy. Other voices within him said, "Seek simplicity. Seek obscurity. God must increase and you must decrease." He remembered Servant Jonathan's frequent admonition, "Do good and disappear." A verse from Ecclesiastes came to convict him, "Do not be excessively righteous and do not be overly wise."

"I thank you for your offer, Gorbon Kreeg, but I must turn you down. The Lord has other, less sensational plans for me. My heart yearns to live in obscurity," the little monk explained.

Gorbon Kreeg's eyes narrowed into two pinpoints of cold darkness, then he spit out a warning. "You will be sorry that you did not become my disciple, little monk, very sorry. No one turns down Gorbon Kreeg and still has a day of peace. I have my ways and I have friends in high places, particularly a judge you've offended lately."

Gorbon Kreeg hastily gathered together his disciples and congratulated them on their performance that day. The remaining crowd of people cheered them as they moved through the narrow streets of the village and out the gate. He looked back with greed. "The village is mine," he declared in a low, victorious hiss.

The little monk went to the doorway of an abandoned building, slid down onto the stone steps worn by centuries of passersby and pulled his robe up over his head to seek God in the inner temple of his soul. He wanted God to touch the uneasiness of his heart about the promises—and warning—from Gorbon Kreeg. "O God, speak, for your servant is listening."

The little monk centered himself down in silence, waiting for the voice of God to speak its thunderous wisdom. But, he heard only a still, small voice. Then he heard the voice say, "Go fishing." The words seemed out of place and hardly what he expected from the God of all things. "Go fishing," said the voice again. So the little monk went fishing. He broke a hole in the ice. It was not in his nature, though, to harm any living thing, so he put no hook on his line—only bread for bait. He tossed out his fishing line and washed his face in the icy water. If this were summer, he thought, minnows would be swimming around my toes. In the middle of winter, summer always seems so far away.

He remembered the words of Gregory of Nazianzus, "Study fish."

17. Pray As You Can, Not As You Can't

Winter still held Maloo in its fierce grip. The voice of the turtledove had not yet been heard in the land. The little monk stood in an open field surveying the frozen acres that would soon be turned for spring planting. He talked to a farmer worried about the acres he did not get planted the year before. The little monk tried to point out the abundant harvest the farmer had gotten from the acres he did plant.

A printer approached them and asked the little monk for a conference. The farmer left them in order to go on to other parts of his farm. The little monk noted that the farmer continued to shake his head at the acres he failed to plant in past years.

"Are you the little monk, the one who knows all about prayer?" the printer inquired.

The little monk turned to see a very serious person looking him over from his hooded head to his sandaled feet. "I am the little monk, but I only know a little about prayer—not much. What I do *not* know about prayer is so much greater than what I do know. When one has learned one of prayer's secrets, Father Prayer begets another secret."

"How should I pray?" asked the man. "There are so many methods and plans that I can't keep up with them."

"I can only tell you what one of the prayer masters taught us," answered the little monk. "Pray as you can, not as you can't. Pray on the basis of what you already know.

"The little monk turned to see a very serious person..."

That's more than enough to take you into the kingdom of God."

"I have a question for you," the printer said. "Why do I feel so isolated and alone when I pray? Sometimes I feel like I'm the only one praying, even though I know that's not true. My single prayer seems to be but a tiny, dim star in a galaxy of glimmering planets, moons and suns. Is God really listening to my one prayer? Doesn't my little prayer get lost in the travel from earth to heaven?"

"No prayer stands alone," said the little monk. "Every single prayer is linked to every other prayer ever prayed by any believer from any age. Your prayer is another link, but an important one, in the great chain of prayer that connects heaven and earth, time and eternity, the church and her Lord in one grand communion of the saints."

"I never thought of it that way," the printer said.

"Your prayer is part of a seamless robe sewn from all of the prayers of God's people, something woven into the fabric of faithful devotion of the church universal. Every prayer exists as part of the family of prayer. Noah prayed. Abraham prayed. Joseph prayed. The prophets prayed. David prayed. Jesus prayed. The disciples prayed. Paul prayed. Augustine prayed. The martyrs prayed. And you pray. Your prayer is heard by a cloud of witnesses so great that no one can number them."

"Our prayers live on, then?" asked the printer.

"Yes, very much so," the little monk responded. "The giants of prayer taught that true prayers are forever. They never die. They outlive the lives of those who uttered them; outlive a generation, outlive an age, outlive the world. Every prayer has the seed of eternity in it.

"The apostle John, in the eighth chapter of his Revelation, described a great scene in which an angel mixes incense with the prayers of all the saints and the incense and the prayers go up before the Lord.

"Most Christians think that Christianity began the day they became a Christian," said the little monk. "But Christianity is two thousand years old. When you are reborn, you are reborn in the church, in the midst of believers, the body of Christ. When you were converted, you were converted to the Christ who is Lord of the church. Your prayers, then, are offered as part of the whole church praying, as it has prayed and worshiped for two thousand years. The church praying is a great spiritual tapestry in which your own prayers are an important thread in the whole design."

The printer left in peace. As the months inched by, the printer's life overflowed with a river of prayer from heavenly Jerusalem itself, the mother of us all. Stories began to circulate about his praying. Those who overheard him pray often said that when he prayed, saints in their graves turned over in order to hear better, so true were the man's prayers.

"He has found the monk within him," the little monk said.

18. Shy? Why?

*O*ne day at the village well in Maloo, as the little monk looked into its depth for wisdom and guidance, a merchant came over to him.

"Little monk, can you help me?" the merchant asked.

The little monk took notice of this quiet, retiring man. "What kind of help do you need? It looks to me like the world has treated you in friendly ways."

"Yes, that's the way I analyze it, too. But that's the problem. I analyze every single thing, pick it to pieces, turn it over and over again in my mind until there's not a shred of good left in the thing. I'm incurably given to introspection. I'm not satisfied until I have peeled back the last possible meaning of anything that happens to me. You see, I'm shy."

"Shyness can be the door to despair. These two, shyness and looking within, feed off each other, each one contributing to the anguish of the other. Shyness can often lead to isolation, lack of focus and a feeling of lovelessness," explained the little monk. "There is no dungeon as dark as that which surrounds the shy person."

"Can you help me?" the merchant asked. "I'm afraid to meet with my customers. I'm barely even making a living as a merchant. And customers frighten me to death. I mumble when I talk. Mumblers don't sell much."

"I think you should remember that many of the Bible heroes were shy. Moses tried to turn down leading the children of Israel because he was not eloquent. Saul came from the smallest tribe, Gideon from a poor family, Jeremiah argued that he was too young, David was a poor man of low esteem, Elijah was frightened. All these heroes were shy, for the most part."

"I hadn't realized that," replied the merchant.

"You're in good company, if you're shy. You should also remember that most people are shy some time or other. But it's no fun to be shy, for then, when you meet people, you're timid and quiet. The shy rarely share ideas or feelings. They're easily embarrassed and have little zest for life," explained the little monk.

"I feel so invisible. I feel like a prisoner that no one wants to visit," said the merchant.

"You are only a prisoner in your mind. When you become a prisoner of the cross, a prisoner of Christ, you will be free in every respect. Shyness makes us hide our talents and hide our life. But the kingdom of God calls us to grow. Shyness robs us of the freedom to grow and to love," taught the little monk.

"I want to be free, I want to engage life, I want energy and boldness to flow through me," the merchant decided.

"Then make it your prayer to do so. Let me give you a life verse from Paul's counsel to his disciple, Timothy: 'God has not given us a spirit of timidity, but of power and love and self-control.'

"Now, let me tell you a story about one of the lost secrets of Nineveh," he added.

"The king of Nineveh had a son who was...well, different. He was sort of sickly, yet not really sick. He was sort of strange, yet not really so. Mainly he was shy, bashful and withdrawn. He never said a word in public. Besides that, he was always running into things because he was so preoccupied with himself.

"The king brought in all sorts of doctors, astrologers and magicians to see if they could find a cure. In spite of

"He was always running into things…"

all the incantations, spells and potions, the king's son only got worse.

"The king was very worried, both for his son's health, but also, since the son was an only child, that there might not be a competent heir to the throne. The king once wept openly about the possibility of his kingdom coming to an end, all because his son was shy and afraid of people. His son needed a special gift.

"Finally, the king put up a large reward for anyone who could help his son. People lined up in droves to offer help. 'Rub him with lizard oil,' said one. 'Pull all of his teeth,' another suggested. 'Soak his feet in goats' milk three times a day,' offered a village person. 'Make him learn Latin; that will cure him,' a dignitary from another kingdom advised. 'Let him eat grasshoppers and honey,' the town mayor said, based on a family cure handed down for centuries. And so it went.

"Now, it wasn't that the boy was ignorant. In fact, he was very bright, good at his studies and quick to learn new things. He could spell *Zerubbabel* and *Jehosophat* without missing a letter.

"One day, a servant passed by the door to the son's room. He heard a strong voice delivering a speech. The servant recognized the speech since it was the one that the king himself had delivered earlier that day. The servant thought that perhaps the king was in the son's room and was reviewing his speech for his son. Cautiously, the servant pushed open the door, but was amazed to see that it was the son giving the speech out loud to himself, pacing from one end of the richly decorated room to the other.

"The servant was awed by the transformation in the son when he was pretending to be his father, the king. The moment the son saw the servant, he ran to hide himself behind a high armoire.

"'No, no,' said the servant. 'Your speech was good, very good.'

"'But it was my father's speech.'

"'Better to give your father's speech than no speech at all.'

"'Why can I give a speech when I imitate my father but not when I'm myself?' asked the son.

"'Because you gaze in the wrong direction,' replied the servant.

"'What does that mean?'

"'It means, my lord, that you are gazing at yourself. Gazing at ourselves makes us shrink and look smaller in our own eyes. When we take our eyes off ourselves and gaze at others, we grow large, not only in the eyes of others, but in our own eyes as well. Gaze at the goodness in others and you will stand taller than the tallest person in the kingdom.'

"'But how do I see this goodness in others?' asked the king's son.

"'You see it mirrored in their eyes,' answered the servant. 'If you look deep enough into the eyes of others you will see souls wanting to reach out to meet you because without you they are incomplete. Without you they do not have one of the pieces that makes them whole. By withholding yourself, you rob others of completion and wholeness. Is that what you want to do? This is a lesson we can all learn well: Gaze at God and gaze into the hearts of others and you'll have no time nor desire to gaze at yourself. The psalmist said of God, "I long to gaze on you in the sanctuary."'

"Whoever spends time looking only at self will find that analyzing oneself becomes a habit. Too much looking inward makes us addicted to our own feelings of inadequacy," concluded the little monk. "Think about this. If you were dying of thirst, would you go to an empty bucket or to a bucket filled with fresh, cool water just drawn from a deep well? If you always look within, you'll only find an empty bucket. Go to God's deepest well and you will receive abundantly of that which gives life. The upward look and the outward look fill our empty selves to over-flowing and heals the shyness within. God gives boldness in abundance."

"I want to gaze on God. I want to gaze on the hearts of others," said the merchant with conviction.

"You have the passion to change. That's most of the bat-tle," replied the little monk. "In the least expected places of her writings, Hildegard of Bingen used to say, 'Passion is the answer.'"

"One last question. Where do I find the nearest well?" the merchant asked, smiling awkwardly.

"Right beside you," said the little monk, lowering an empty bucket into the deep well near where they were standing. When he pulled up the first full bucket it splashed over its sides and made them both as wet as a summer rain.

19. The Return of the Shepherd

*O*n bended knees, the little monk picked up leaves from the stone path leading to the chapel.

As he knelt there he realized that he himself had brought much of this stone from the riverbed and had crushed it with a large hammer and scattered it along the path. Sometimes paths are given to us in life and sometimes we make our own paths in the journey with God, thought the little monk.

He often made a game of work. He sorted the wet, withering leaves into three piles—those that had turned to rot, those with enough beauty still in them to catch the fancy of leaf-gathering children, and those whose beauty had only faded some.

Suddenly, he shivered from a growing sense of an unknown presence.

A long shadow fell over him. He turned quickly, his eyes peering at a figure bending over him. He recognized the shepherd from an earlier meeting. The little monk sighed with relief.

"Shepherd, you startled me," said the little monk. "Why are you here?"

"May we walk and talk?" asked the shepherd.

The little monk hesitated about leaving his work behind, but decided to go ahead and walk with the shepherd.

They went off the stone path, out the gate and toward the cemetery. They walked among the simple gravestones, all

"A long shadow fell over him."

alike, all bearing only a name, birth date and date of death. The little monk glanced around at the sea of monks who had all struggled with the same issue—to learn how to pray without ceasing. He felt at home here among these silent witnesses. Standing in the center of this great carpet of sleeping saints, the little monk asked again, "What do you want with me?"

"I have come to give you the gift, as I promised," said the shepherd.

"Shepherd, I told you before. I need nothing. I have all I need here at the monastery," replied the little monk.

"Well, then, for now, let me offer you two other small gifts," spoke the shepherd.

How ironic for this poor shepherd to be offering gifts, thought the little monk. Still, he wondered what the shepherd had in mind.

"Here," said the shepherd, holding out a closed fist. The little monk held out his hand, palm up. The shepherd placed a tiny object in his hand. "A hazelnut!" the little monk said aloud.

But the shepherd became distracted by a lamb passing by. It had wandered away from its mother. He hoisted the lamb in his arms and returned it to its mother not far away.

In the meantime, the little monk pondered the meaning of the hazelnut. His thoughts quickly went to something he had read a few days ago in his holy reading time. It was a passage by Julian of Norwich in *The Revelations of Divine Love.* He had copied the passage in his journal. He asked if he could read it to the shepherd. One by one, the words of the passage rolled off the little monk's lips:

And in this he showed me something small, no bigger than a hazelnut, lying in the palm of my hand, as it seemed to me, and it was round as a ball. I looked at it with the eye of my understanding and thought: What can this be? I was amazed that it could last, for I thought that because of its littleness it would suddenly have fallen into nothing. And I was answered in my understanding: It lasts and always will, because God loves it: and thus everything has being through the love of God. In this little thing I saw three properties. The first is that God made it, the second is that God loves it, the third is that God preserves it. But what did I see in it? It is that God is the Creator and the protector and the lover. For until I am substantially united to him, I can never have perfect rest or true happiness, until, that is, I am so attached to him that there can be no created thing between God and me.

The little monk held the hazelnut in his clenched fist as if he were holding a big truth. Then he placed it in his pocket where he always carried some seeds; a small, smooth stone; and a lovely leaf or two.

"Now for my second small gift," said the shepherd, "A story."

The little monk loved stories, for they always taught him a new truth. Stories are the stuff of life, he told himself. He sat down under the copper beech tree, gathered Purr onto his lap, for she loved stories too, and settled into listening to the shepherd's story.

"Once upon a time, there was a man who was known as the silliest man in the valley. There seemed to be no end to the silly things he would do, such as taking a bath in the snow, kissing pigs on the mouth, giving away any money whenever he got it—all the things one should not do.

"Well, one day, a bright idea hit him. He would go to see the king. The very next day, he set out on his journey with a loaf of bread and three turnips and a wineskin.

"As he went on his way, he met a chicken who asked, 'Where are you going?'

"'I am going to see the king,' answered the silly man. 'May I join you?' asked the chicken. 'Certainly,' answered the silly man.

"Then he met a goat who asked, 'Where are you going?'

"'Soon. Very soon. I am going to see the king,' answered the silly man again. 'I will go, too,' replied the goat.

"A horse noticed the three of them and said, 'Where are you going in such a hurry?'

"'I am going to see the king,' replied the silly man in all seriousness. 'And so are we,' replied the animals.

"A bird came flying by and landed on the horse's back. 'Where are you going?' asked the bird.

"'Soon. Very soon. I am going to see the king,' said the silly man, time and time again, to the gathering crowd of animals who joined his train.

"As he came into village after village, a parade of people watched the silly man and all the animals passing by. 'Where are you going?' they asked.

"'I am going to see the king,' he would reply.

"'That's silly,' they mocked and jeered. 'No one just goes to see the king. You must be invited.'

"But still the silly man journeyed onward.

"Finally they reached the forest of the king and decided to rest for the night.

"The king was a lonely king, for he had no sons or daughters.

"Bright and early the next morning, the king decided to indulge in that which gave him great pleasure—hunting.

He filled his quiver full of arrows and headed for the forest. Some princes and guards went with him.

"A chicken moved in the clearing. The king thought it was a pheasant and shot his strongest, straightest arrow in that direction. At that moment, the silly man stepped into the clearing and the arrow went through his shoulder, just missing his heart.

"'Oh, I have shot me a man,' cried the king. They rushed to the side of the man, as he lay bleeding upon the ground. His eyes flickered and he mumbled, 'I have seen the king. Let me die now.' But the king would not let him die. 'Gather him up and bring his friends of the forest with him. This day he will become my son. This day he will become a child of the king.' Though all the world had considered this man to be silly, the king loved him, adopted him and took him into the castle and shared all his bounty with the silly man.

"The silly man almost died of his wounds, but the king kept him alive. With great difficulty the doctors were able to remove the arrow. Throughout the rest of his days, the wound would always have some pain to it, but the silly man simply dismissed it as his 'wound of love.'"

While the little monk took in the meaning of the story, the shepherd said, "I must be going now." Sternly, he looked into the little monk's eyes and said, "Be on your watch for Gorbon Kreeg. The whole village seems to have turned his way. He's doing miracles now and some have called him another Elijah; others, John the Baptist anew. But listen, Gorbon Kreeg also has been asking pointed questions about you in the community. Don't say too much. Sometimes silence is the greater language anyway. Even the truth can be twisted by a man like that. A parable or a proverb could be held against you."

This warning issued, the shepherd left as quietly as he had come.

The little monk picked up his empty bucket and got down on his knees to gather more leaves. "Now, there's a beauty," he said, pushing it into his pocket. When he shoved it to the bottom of his pocket, he brushed against the hazelnut and the love of God surged within him.

20. Prayer Is a Pearl of Great Price

On one crisp, frosty day late in winter, the little monk stood at the edge of the marketplace teaching about the origins of prayer.

"Prayer is one of the great mysteries of the universe. We must never forget that prayer preceded recorded scripture, yet must always be done in accord with scripture. Noah, Abraham, Jacob and Moses—all prayed before the scriptures were ever written. In that sense prayer was the oldest sacrament by which God released his grace in the lives of people. Prayer was the first sacrament—the outward sign of an inward working of God."

The little monk continued his instruction. "Prayer is a great mystery. God knows all, thinks all, creates all, plans all, yet calls us mere monks of everyday life to build the kingdom of God through prayer. In a way, God commands us to pray as if all really depended on our prayers. Yet, in the end, everything depends on him. For God's own reason, he has chosen prayer to be the tool by which much of his will is to be worked out in the world. That's why his house, his dwelling place, is to be called a house of prayer."

"Why is prayer so hard?" asked a villager.

"Because the natural leaning of our hearts is to want quick answers," responded the little monk. "The flesh resists spiritual work. The desert fathers used to talk about the *work* of prayer, meaning that it demanded intense effort

"'Why is prayer so hard?' asked a villager."

from us. Do not be mistaken. Prayer is work—disciplined, sweaty, hard work. Yet never was work more joyous. The hard work of prayer is heavy on the flesh but light on the spirit. The scriptures say that God's commands are not heavy. The command to pray is not a heavy burden to the soul, only to the flesh."

Some of the villagers became uneasy and started to drift off to more interesting things going on in the marketplace. These sayings of the little monk were becoming too difficult for them. Others called him, "Little Socrates," since he traveled about sharing his teachings as philosophers often do.

"I've noticed that the reason I don't pray as much as I should is the constancy of prayer, its perpetual dailiness," remarked a curious banker holding on to his money bag lest it be stolen in the crowd gathered to hear this street teacher. "Paul's words, 'Pray without ceasing,' are so simple yet so hard to do," the banker continued. "To pray in that way would be to give my whole life over to prayer. I would have to turn my life inside out, and start over again."

"Yes, prayer is radical," answered the little monk. "Prayer is revolutionary. More than one revolution has been started by the simple act of folding the hands together in prayer. Strong, powerful, constant prayer gathers all of life into a new spiritual mosaic. Nothing remains untouched by Mother Prayer. As a human mother becomes totally involved in the life of her children, even so does Mother Prayer involve herself in every area of our lives. The power of prayer is bone-deep.

"In the seventeenth century, George Herbert left us with these beautiful words about the vast sweep of prayer. The images and metaphors keep piling up in the poem:

Prayer, the Church's banquet, Angels' age,
  God's breath in man returning to his birth,
The soul in paraphrase, heart in pilgrimage.
  The Christian plummet, sounding heav'n and earth,
Engine against th' Almighty, sinner's tower,
  Reversèd thunder, Christ-side-piercing spear,
The Six-days' world transposing in an hour,
  A kind of tune, which all things hear and fear;
Softness, and peace, and joy, and love, and bliss,
  Exalted manna, gladness of the best,
Heaven in ordinary, man well drest,
  The milky way, the bird of Paradise,
Church-bells beyond the stars heard, the soul's blood,
  The land of spices; something understood.

"Prayer is a pearl of great price," said the little monk. "Prayer is free, but it costs a lot."

"What does that mean?" asked the merchant, puzzled that something could be free and costly at the same time.

"Prayer is a gift freely offered by the Holy Spirit. But to use the gift as God intended, that will cost you everything. Prayer always asks more of us. Prayer asks us to become more than we are."

"Those are profound things to be considered," answered the merchant. "Only the learned should hear them. These things cannot be understood by the ordinary person. Perhaps we should gather the intellectuals together and teach them so that they, in turn, can teach the common folk. You know, start a new religion," said the merchant. "Maybe you should become a disciple of the prophet Gorbon Kreeg. He's turned the village to new ways of thinking about God. You'd make a good disciple of his."

"Would you like to hear a parable?" the little monk asked.

"Can we understand it?" the merchant asked.

"Parables are for the spiritual ones. Spiritual people have no difficulty understanding parables, for parables are always spoken in the plain language of the kingdom of God.

"This, then, is the parable," noted the little monk.

"A very famous playwright decided to produce a play. What do I need for my play to succeed, he thought to himself. He talked to architects and theater managers, artists and actors. When he was done, he had gotten to what he thought was the core element of theater. He stripped away the building and costumes and lighting. He discovered that he could produce his play in a park. People could sit on the hillocks. The stars, the moon and a few torches could light the play. All that was needed for theater to succeed was an eight-foot open space, a few actors and actresses, a good story and a passion or two.

"This is the teaching of the parable," the little monk continued. "The great things of life can be reduced to a few basics. So it is with prayer. The mystery of prayer can be grasped in its simplicity, so that prayer is not an elaborate, ornamental thing, but something so basic that a child or an unlearned, homeless stranger could easily learn to do it with great effect on the soul."

The marketplace crowd thinned out even more at this point, leaving only some basket weavers, a few children, a furniture maker, a young mother and the village reprobate to ponder the eternal significance of these words.

Even on this cold-lingering day, a swallow tried to get an early start on spring by picking up some twigs to start a new nest.

"Prayer is as practical as potatoes," the little monk concluded. "Prayer is as simple as that swallow over there."

Some of the people chuckled to themselves about this as they watched the swallow engage in life at its most basic, hunting for worms, the "daily bread" of birds.

They all left before the little monk added, "Prayer is a strong knock on heaven's door."

21. The Loneliest Woman in the World

*T*he little monk received a letter from a famous musician who described herself as "the loneliest woman in the world."

In spite of fame and fortune, she had no close friends, she wrote. "If I were to die today, I'm absolutely persuaded that no one would come to my funeral," she said.

The woman indicated that she would be traveling through the area and would like to stop and see the little monk. He sought the abbot's permission, then wrote her and encouraged her to come.

She arrived in Maloo on a dreary day. Dark, heavy clouds wrestled with each other in an ugly sky. Her mood sunk lower with each roll of spiteful thunder and downpour of relentless rain.

The little monk offered her a steaming cup of tea and some biscuits with honey. They sat before a mellow fire, gentle to the bones and soothing to the soul.

"Why is there such loneliness in the world?" she asked. "Why is there this everlasting yearning for friends and fellowship?"

"Some say that people are lonely because they build barricades rather than bridges," answered the little monk.

"Is that the only explanation?" the woman asked.

"Some say that loneliness is in the eye of the beholder. What one person calls the pain of loneliness, another calls the glory and joy of solitude," the little monk added.

"The loneliest woman in the world"

"But what do you say, little monk?" asked the woman.

"Our loneliness is really not a desire for people, but for God. I've always thought of the lonely as born with a piece of themselves left behind with the almighty Father. Our loneliness can never be filled until we rejoin ourselves with that piece of us still held by our Father in heaven. The piece that was left behind is that part of us which is our greatest longing—intimacy with God. We can fill that emptiness temporarily with other people, but fellowship with the Father is our real desire.

"The lonely are often ready for a deep relationship with God," the little monk said.

The loneliest woman in the world discovered that while she seemed deficient in relating at the human level, she was abundantly capable of intimacy with God, that her ache for human contact was really an ache for encounter with the divine.

"I've found three friends tonight," the woman said. "A little monk, myself—and God."

"The place that is weakest in us, the point of deep despair, is always where we find the monk within us, the spiritual serenity that makes us whole," added the little monk.

He picked up another log and put it on the fire. Purr left her usual place by the fireside in order to nap on the woman's lap. The woman rubbed Purr's furry back. Purr yawned, then the woman and finally the little monk himself. Such yawns come only from contented monks.

The fire popped and crackled. A hot ember dropped to the bottom of the fireplace and glowed far into the night.

22. Come Play the Game of Minutes

*T*he little monk went to work in the kitchen in place of one of the brothers who had taken ill. When he arrived at the door to the kitchen, rather than being greeted with the smell of fresh bread baking, he heard nothing but the noise from pans being thrown.

One of the monks who had been assigned to the kitchen some months ago was having a fit—a real rampage. The little monk was not used to such clatter and noise breaking the sacred atmosphere of the monastery. The other monk could not give up on his fit. His fury continued and would not be constrained.

The little monk decided that the situation called for some humor. He stood in the middle of the kitchen holding up his cross as one does to ward off the curse of Dracula. At first the little monk's action made the brother only more furious, but finally the brother broke down laughing and fell to the floor holding his sides in convulsive heaves of laughter. Then he sat up and became very serious again.

"I'm leaving the monastery, you know," said the brother.

"Why?" asked the little monk.

"Because I hate this kitchen work. I became a monk in order to pray and to meditate and to contemplate, not to cook and wash dishes. Six hours a day I spend working here. When some of the brothers get sick, I work even longer. I have no time left for prayer. At night I fall asleep

139

"One of the monks was having a fit."

when first I open the scriptures. This morning I fell asleep in the middle of the singing of the psalms. My spiritual life is slipping away. I want to go to another monastery where I can find God again."

"Better to find God here in the kitchen of Maloo than at a monastery that is noted for being an easy place to find God," responded the little monk.

"What do you mean?"

"*The Rule of St. Benedict* says: 'For they are truly monks when they live by the labor of their hands as did our fathers and the apostles,'" the little monk instructed.

"But kitchen work has to be the least spiritual kind of work," replied the brother.

"Have you not heard of Brother Lawrence and his small book, *The Practice of the Presence of God?*" asked the little monk.

"No, tell me please," replied the brother.

"Brother Lawrence was converted at the age of eighteen by the mere sight, surprisingly, of a dead-looking, leafless tree shivering in the crusted snow of winter. He was stirred within by the profound change that God would bring to that barren tree when spring arrived. From that moment on he fell in love with the God who could also transform his own life. He joined the barefoot Carmelites of Paris," explained the little monk.

"But what has that got to do with me?" asked the brother.

"Well, for fifteen years he worked in the monastery kitchen, doing what he called 'little things for the love of God.' In the hurry of the kitchen he learned to keep himself calm and collected, doing each thing in its season with uninterrupted tranquility, by practicing the presence of Christ."

The little monk took out his journal, worn by the years of use, the journal where he had mined golden nuggets from the wisdom of those pioneers of the spirit who, through the ages, had conquered spiritual frontiers. He turned to favorite comments of Brother Lawrence: "Were I a preacher, I should above all things, preach the practice of the presence of God....He requires no great matters of us: a little remembrance of him from time to time, a little adoration; sometimes to pray for his grace, sometimes to offer him your sufferings, and sometimes to return him thanks for the favors he has given you, and still gives you, in the midst of your troubles....Lift up your heart to him...the least little remembrance will always be acceptable to him. You need not cry very loud; he is nearer to us than we are aware of."

The little monk read some more: "The time of business does not with me differ from the time of prayer; and in the noise and clatter of my kitchen, while several persons are at the same time calling for different things, I possess God in as great tranquility as if I were upon my knees at the blessed sacrament."

"That's a remarkable idea," responded the brother.

"Yes, to live in the presence of Christ no matter what the outer circumstance, as Brother Lawrence said, is 'the glorious employment of a Christian, it's our profession.'"

"Is it possible," asked the brother, "to live in the presence of Christ all the time? Is it really possible for a human being to dwell so close to Christ, to have that kind of intimate relationship—or have we been fooled all along by religious zealots?"

"Theophan the Recluse put it very bluntly," the little monk noted: "'The awareness of God shall be with you as clearly as a toothache.'"

The brother liked that statement, remembering how persistent a toothache is whether one is talking, reading, working or sleeping. There is no way of escaping the ache.

"When one has achieved living in the presence of Christ continually, one always has a slight ache for God," the little monk said, smiling. "Richard of Chichester used to pray, 'O Most Merciful Friend, Brother and Redeemer; May I know thee more clearly, love thee more dearly, and follow thee more nearly.'"

"But don't we have to concentrate on external things while we're doing them? How can I concentrate on these things and on Christ at the same time?" inquired the brother.

"Meister Eckhart explained, 'As thou art in church or cell, that same frame of mind carry out into the world, into its turmoil and its fitfulness.' The Quakers teach that deep within us all there is an inner sanctuary, a holy place, a divine center, a secret hermitage, a remote retreat, a tent hidden in the wilderness to which we may return again and again, even in the midst of the hustle and bustle of daily life. Through a process the Quakers call 'centering down,' we can quiet our souls, even when surrounded by furious activity, and do it so well that we can actually live on two levels at once, one earthly, the other heavenly. To practice the perpetual presence of Christ is to pray without ceasing," said the little monk.

"Let these pots and pans become together a holy grail for you," added the little monk.

The brother had much to think about. The little monk picked up several pots and pans scattered over the kitchen floor and began to put order to the kitchen. The brother watched for a moment, then began to help, touching each violated utensil as if it had become a vessel in the Lord's temple. The little monk picked up a biscuit from the floor, dusted away a few flecks of dirt, broke it in two, gave the top half, the choice part, to the brother and placed the wafer-thin bottom in his own mouth.

"You see, to practice the presence of Christ is to play the game of minutes," said the little monk. "See how many minutes of each day you can keep God in the forefront of your mind. To do so more minutes each day is to win the game of minutes."

From that day on, even though the brother worked in the kitchen for years, one heard only the sound of a song as he worked with the pots and pans. As Brother Lawrence did, he too became the friend of pots and pans. He gave each of them a name.

At the end of every day, the last entry in the brother's journal simply recorded the number of minutes he had captured for God that day.

23. God Is Only a Prayer Away

"**W**hy is life so difficult?" a poor man asked.

"Where is God when I really need him?" another villager asked.

"Why do so few good things ever happen to me?" someone else pondered in despair.

These were the hard questions often brought to the little monk.

In private, some of the monks of the monastery, though cell-broken from the habits and attitudes of the world, still brought similar kinds of questions.

"The more I pray, the more God seems to be absent. Why is that?"

"Does God know how hard it is, on some days, to believe?"

"Why is God so silent when my unbelief and doubt are so noisy?"

The little monk had no answers for them except to murmur, "No spare days."

"What does that mean?" they asked.

"In our life with God, there are no spare days, no days untouched by his grace. Every day is a grace day, no matter how harsh, how dark, how cruel.

"George Herbert, the English poet, wrote these words, so full of truth:

145

"'Why is life so difficult?' a poor man asked."

Thou that hast given so much to me,
Give one thing more, a grateful heart...
Not thankful when it pleaseth me,
As if thy blessings had spare days
But such a heart whose pulse may be thy praise."

The little monk continued. "These are hard days in which we are called to unrelenting faithfulness and unending trust in God's daily mercies until the joy comes. Our days were all recorded long ago when time was only a thought in the mind of God. The psalmist said: 'In your book were written all the days that were formed for me, when none of them as yet existed.'"

The little monk offered a parable.

"There once was a man who counted his days. That was his delight, to keep count of the days he had lived. He recorded them in a book with the major events listed for each day. One day when he was away on a trip his home burned to the ground. The flames had gobbled up his book of days. When he discovered what had happened, no one could console him. 'My days are gone! My days are gone,' he cried. Depressed for many months, he realized finally that heaven keeps its own journal of our days, and a far better journal it is.

"The man learned that there are no lost days, no wasted days, no spare days unpenetrated by the grace of God. Our days are like the sands of an hourglass except that the days begin, flow and end in God."

"I don't understand," said one of the monks.

The little monk showed them an hourglass made in a special way. He placed on a table a double hourglass, one glass on top of another. When grains of sand fell through from the top to the bottom of one hourglass, they actually went on to fall to the top of the second hourglass, so that the sand already fallen immediately became the sand to come—the past meeting the future.

"Alpha and Omega, beginning and end, are both in God's hands," said the little monk, watching sand fall in the hourglass.

"Make each grain of sand in the hourglass a prayer. Make each tick of the clock a praise to God. Redeem the time. In that way, you play the game of minutes, for God is only a prayer away," he told the monks gathered around the hourglass. "Make good use of this window in time and then there will be no spare days in which God's grace is absent."

24. Too Wounded to Serve

*O*n these Lenten days, the little monk's attention turned often to the deeper things of the cross as they apply to daily life. He thought of those who plow hard fields with broken-down horses or are left to sell Friday's fruit on Monday or who change babies' wet diapers or who simply wonder about things.

During these days, the little monk gave himself to contemplation and meditation, to a leaning toward God, like climbing a hill on a windy day. He enjoyed the Lord's leisure by resting in the palm of God's hand, fasting and walking in the Spirit.

"There is hope for the prisoners of time. Each day, the kingdom of God is in the hands of everyday monks where they work and live," said the little monk.

This was a period in which the little monk grew to understand the crucified life. He involved himself with people, transforming ordinary days into uncommon ones by showing people deep insights into their daily occurrences.

"Life wouldn't be so bad if it wasn't so daily," someone told the little monk.

"But God is very daily, too," the little monk responded.

The little monk worked one day in the shade of a mighty oak tree gathering some of its acorns as gifts for the children. A frail-looking woman approached sadly.

"Help me gather acorns for the children," said the little monk.

"The little monk worked one day in the shade of a mighty oak."

"No," answered the woman. "I'm too weak, too fragile. You don't know the deepness of my wounds."

"Why don't you let go of your woundedness and serve the kingdom of God?"

The woman was startled. "If I let go of my wounds, who would I be?"

What a shame, thought the little monk, that this woman had no identity apart from her woundedness!

So he told her a parable of the kingdom, a tale of hope.

"I once read a child's story called 'The Princess with the Glass Heart.' It seems that once upon a time a princess was born with a glass heart. One day when she was still in her youth, she leaned out of a window to view the world and to take in as much of its beauty as she could. While leaning over the window ledge, she heard something break. It was her heart. All of the great physicians of the land were called in to diagnose the situation. All but one shook his head, indicating no hope. The last physician told them that the princess's heart had not shattered completely, but did have a hairline crack.

"'What can we do?' asked her parents.

"'Nothing,' replied the physician. 'Everyone knows that glass hearts, when broken, never heal.'

"But it seems that the princess lived a long, beautiful life and died full of years by being ever so mindful all her days that she had within her a broken heart. Even with her broken heart she still outlived most of her contemporaries. But more importantly she lived a good life, engaged daily in whatever life brought to her door."

The little monk touched his own wounded hip and said, "A broken heart does not make us weak, only mindful. In spite of our wounds, we can always affirm:

Though I fall from wuthering heights,
love will always catch me.

"Our wounds define the quality of our life only if we allow them to. We have a choice in what our wounds do to us. Day-by-day mindfulness in the careful living of the details of life is the way to gain strength for the difficult journey."

The woman breathed deeply and sighed her woundedness away in a moment of prayer. Then she leaned over to pick up acorns for the children of the village. Purr sat with an acorn in her mouth, waiting for the little monk to see how dutiful she was. He took the acorn from Purr's mouth and scratched behind her ears.

"Our wounds are but a gate to the wisdom of God," said the little monk.

In all her days, the pain never left the woman—but neither did the new joy of God.

25. Guilt Is Not a Pleasant Roommate

*A*t midday there came a knock at the door to the little monk's cell. He was taken quickly outside to the garden.

One of the other monks brought to the little monk a ragged-looking man in the throes of spiritual pain, weak from travel and tired from some sin he could not conquer. The other monk left in silence, his lips moving in unceasing prayer. There was a long pause. The man seemed very uneasy. The two stared at each other, reading depths and mysteries in each other's eyes.

"I have a burden that's crushing me, a sin I committed years and years ago," said the man, wiping the rain and dirt from his face. "I have heard that you are a prayer doctor. That's what I need."

"Have you confessed your sin personally to the Lord? If we confess our sins, he is faithful and just to forgive that sin and to cleanse us from all unrighteousness," the little monk counseled.

"I know that in my mind," the man said, "but I don't ever feel forgiven. I've confessed my sin a thousand times and yet my burden feels a thousand times heavier. Through these eyes of guilt, I see nothing but ugliness in the world. My heart is starved for the beauty of deep down things."

"Then perhaps you need another path of confession," the little monk replied, noticing how battered and tired this man seemed by his own sin.

"One of the other monks brought…a ragged-looking man…"

"I'll do whatever is needed," the man promised.

"Some people find great benefit in sharing with a friend. Find a close, spiritual friend who is strong enough to hear your story and offer counsel.

"Or perhaps you have a spiritual director who will hear your sin and guide you into forgiveness and reconciliation."

"Must one go to a priest or minister?" inquired the man.

"Not at all," responded the little monk, "but don't avoid these appointed ambassadors of God's forgiveness either. There's a wise saying about confessing to the priest that's very helpful: when it comes to confession, all people may; none must; many should—but, regretfully, few do."

"Little monk, will you be my spiritual guide? I have none," said the man, with pleading in his voice.

"I'll do what I can. It's near to impossible to engage the inmost self without some spiritual director. It's too easy for the isolated soul to go astray when struggling between the mystery of sin and the certainty of forgiveness."

Together they read David's confession in the Book of Psalms:

Have mercy on me, O God,
according to your loving-kindness;
according to the multitude of your tender mercies,
blot out my transgressions.
Wash me thoroughly of my iniquity
and cleanse me from my sin.

"I have a parable to tell you. There was a man known throughout the community for his good works. Everyone thought he was a saint, but he knew he was a sinner. Yet the community would not let him be a sinner in their eyes. He would confess his sins in private to God, but any time he attempted to go to his minister to confess or to stand up in the congregation to confess his sinfulness, he was not allowed. He was always stifled by accolades and praise of how great and kind and good he was.

"Now it came to pass that the man was tempted and taken in a hideous sin that scandalized his family, his church and the community. All were dumbfounded and shocked beyond belief. They had never seen such betrayal of trust. Some lost their faith in the church. Many were depressed for months. The community shunned him. He finally went away for a while, carrying his heavy burden of sin.

"A year later he returned to the town a broken man. One Sunday he went to church and at an appropriate time he stood and confessed his sins. People were moved by his honesty and forthrightness. They sensed that if such a sinner could be redeemed, then there might be hope for all of them, too. Finally, they saw him for the sinner that he was. He did much more for people as a repentant sinner than he ever did as an adored saint."

"What does the parable mean?" asked the man.

"It means that the ability to confess our faults one to another is a great gift to us," answered the little monk.

"Jesus is the model for us. He was openly and nakedly crucified for us. That's what happens to us when we confess our sins to each other. Our sin is open and naked before another human being whose estimate of us is very important. Better to have sin crucified now than for it to grow like leprosy. Better to have sin crucified now than for it to be judged later before the throne of the Almighty.

"My own spiritual advisor once told me: 'In admonishing you to confession, I am admonishing you simply to be the Christian you were called to be.' The one who is alone with his sin is utterly and hopelessly alone.

"In the presence of the world, I can only be one who makes mistakes; in the presence of a Christian friend, a priest or a spiritual director, I can dare to be a forgiven sinner.

"No wonder, then," continued the little monk "that some churches have made a sacrament of confession. If confession of sin does not open the gates of grace, nothing will." The little monk added: "Confession is a road with a narrow gate and but one destination—the cross of Christ."

The two friends spent the rest of the night in talk and spiritual direction. Early in the morning the man left, having made a good confession to his new friend. Sun broke over the valley in great abandon as the man walked away in the full stature of a renewed person. The load of sin had been left behind. Another ordinary, common saint had experienced the power of the cross.

The little monk slapped his knees in excitement. "This is going to be a great day!"

For quite some time, he sat in the scriptorium on a chair made of cherry, looking down at an illuminated script in a handwritten Bible more than a thousand years old. He ran his fingers over the beautiful script, hoping some of the truth might rub off on his soul.

He took out his journal and poured thoughts into it from a full heart. An hour passed of honest writing about the poverty of sin and the lavish grace of God. As the last words for this day's journal entry, he wrote a proverb of St. John of the Cross about God's calling in us: "God says, 'He that is near me is near the fire.'"

Such words drove the little monk to contemplation, as his mind surrendered itself to a cloud of pure knowing. Vibrant words, a chant from the Psalms, echoed down the halls of the monastery of Maloo: "In the volume of the book it is written of me, that I should fulfill thy will, O God."

Again he touched the brilliant colors of the illuminated script. Then he remembered a character in Dostoyevsky's *The Idiot* who was mocked for suggesting that we shall be saved by beauty. There's some truth in that idea, thought the little monk. The first beauty we know, he concluded, is the beauty of creation—the mountains, the canyons, the living forests, the rivers and seas around us, the bleeding red sunsets.

Yet, all of this created beauty pales in comparison to the beauty of the gospel message of forgiveness and redemption. Still, as we look though the lens of the gospel, the creation itself takes on an even greater beauty. The beauty of the creation opens our hearts. But, the gospel fills our hearts and expands them to take in even more of God and his creation. Since the little monk had been a potter at one time, his heart had a craving for beauty in any form.

Beauty is the prayer of the eye, concluded the little monk.

From that day forward, the little monk knew the sovereignty of God in all things as if it were a truth that hung from every tree in the land.

26. A True Friend Holds Us Accountable

*T*he end of Lent lay just around the corner. The long winter and the austere Lent made the monks of Maloo restless. No wonder, then, that something broke the peace of Maloo. Moods were tense, relationships stale. Then controversy unleashed itself.

One particular brother seemed to be at the center of the turmoil. He had been listening keenly to the new ideas of Gorbon Kreeg and had embraced these ideas in their entirety, without sifting them and measuring them against the scriptures. He also tried to foist the new teaching on others on the grounds that it would increase their spiritual devotion. Debates and arguments increased, interrupting the peace of the monastery. Under the unscrupulous maneuverings of Gorbon Kreeg, the village was being set against the monastery.

"These teachings contaminate the foundation principles upon which this monastery stands," the abbot warned.

But just as critical was the fact that this very brother had been avoiding his spiritual director, with comments that the director didn't understand the new teaching, just as the people of Jesus' day didn't understand Jesus' teaching. What would have happened to Jesus, had he been subject to a human spiritual director, the brother wanted to know.

"Dismiss him," some of the brothers said. "Listen to him," others said, being very open to these new teachings.

*"One particular brother seemed to be at the
center of the turmoil."*

"Discipline him," others called. There was a tear in the holy veil of Maloo.

The wayward brother sought out the little monk for advice.

They decided to go for a walk. What better place to walk and talk and listen than in the midst of God's other creation—the woods and valleys just beyond the monastery.

"Why is everyone so upset with me?" asked the brother.

"Because you teach counter to the accepted teachings and want everyone else to live by the new teachings you've found," replied the little monk. "Listen to this parable."

"One day a rooster in the barnyard proclaimed that each animal should choose a belief and then live and die by that belief. Each animal was to think about this for five days and then make a decision.

"A pig decided that it loved a good roll in the mud and therefore all baths should be taken in mud. A hawk decided that flying gave one a whole new perspective on things. Therefore, flying would be the key to the belief system by which all should live. A duck took great delight in swimming and ducking under water. Swimming had to be a supreme commitment for the duck, so the duck thought. A chicken considered the subject a great deal and quickly decided that eating corn was just about as good as things can get. So corn eating became the supreme doctrine taught by the chicken. A fish quickly made its decision—everyone must be able to live *in* the water.

"Each animal set out to persuade others that their belief was the correct one. However, great problems occurred when the converts took their new beliefs to extremes. The pig killed itself jumping off a cliff, trying to learn to fly. The hawk rolled in mud and found its feathers and wings too clogged to fly. The duck persuaded no one. It was satisfied to hold to its belief in swimming, even though the rest of the world did not seem to care. The fish died with corn caught in its gills. And the chicken drowned trying to swim under water."

"What does your parable mean, little monk?" asked the brother.

"Choose your extremes carefully. They could cost you a greater price than you're willing to pay. The teachings of Gorbon Kreeg do not come cheaply."

"But I really believe the things I'm teaching," the brother asserted.

"I know you do, but the mind can easily go astray if there's no one to whom you're accountable. More than the doctrine, it is the way you're proceeding. Because of the fallenness of our minds, we all need a good friend to counsel us, a spiritual guide, someone to whom we are accountable at the level of the heart, mind and spirit.

"Every spiritual guide needs a spiritual guide as well. No one stands alone. No Christian, however holy, is an island of solitary righteousness. St. Augustine noted, 'No one can walk without a guide.' Remember the Ethiopian eunuch and Philip. Concerning the scripture the eunuch was reading, Philip asked, 'Do you understand these things?' The eunuch replied, 'How can I unless someone guides me.'"

"So without some good friend with whom I can try out new thoughts or attitudes, I can easily go astray," concluded the brother.

"We all can," said the little monk. "We need the wisdom of the word of God and the teaching of the Spirit to hold us to sound doctrine. I remember the words of Theophan the Recluse: 'For avoidance of error, have someone to advise you—a spiritual father or confessor, a brother of like mind; and make known to him all that happens to you in the work of prayer.'

"There is great danger in doing, thinking and believing what one wants. Self-direction leads to pride, error, temptation, deception and self-will. The cure of souls is always done in the context of a supportive, corrective community. Stubborn independence in the body of believers can easily destroy the body and its mission to center on the death of Christ. To talk with oneself is to breathe the same hot air. We need the refreshing winds of dialogue, the truth of the scriptures and the counsel of good guides."

"What should I do?" the brother asked.

"Find a true listener, not someone who is eager to give advice. Sometimes no advice is best. But make up your mind always to be accountable."

"Do you think the brothers will forgive me? How bold of me to think that I alone would have the truth," noted the brother.

"I'm sure they'll forgive you. Especially if they see that you are teachable and are responding to a spiritual counselor," replied the little monk.

"Brother Sigmund is my appointed spiritual guide," said the brother.

"Go seek him out, then," replied the little monk quietly.

The walk ended, and, with his heart right, the brother returned to the monastery ready to work and worship in accountable ways within the life of the community.

The little monk encouraged him to seize the eucharistic moment.

"What's that?" asked the brother.

"There are certain defining moments when we can boldly apply the death of Christ to our situation in life," replied the little monk.

Grateful for an opportunity to return to his cell, the little monk entered the barren room he loved because it was a tool that led him to God. He sat on the edge of the cot and heard the straw rustle. He remembered the day he built his bed. Every monk at Maloo, eventually, had to build the furnishings for his room—the bed, the chair, the table, the nightstand.

He rubbed the deep patina of the oak out of which his nightstand was made. On the nightstand sat a vase he had made when he was an apprentice potter. He took the vase in his hands, knowing that he held his old life between his fingers. Looking back, but only for a moment, he said, "Good," and returned the vase to its proper place in his room and in his mind.

Then he picked up his Bible to read, to engage in one of a monk's great occupations—contemplative reading or *lectio divina,* as it's called—that is, to read scripture until it comes alive in one's heart, driving the imagination and spirit into communion with God.

He remembered the instruction of Brother Stephen: *Lectio divina* is a deeper way to pray. In it, one reads the scriptures slowly, passionately and out loud until a gate in the heart swings open to the frontiers of paradise where, letting go of mind, heart, senses and earthbound images of the holy, there is nothing left for the heart and mind to do but to reach out and grasp God as he is in eternity.

But before the little monk had gone very far this day in divine reading, he noticed that someone had placed a strange bookmark in his Bible—a feather from the tail of a peacock. He looked around to see if anything else in his cell had been disturbed. Nothing. He went out into the common room and asked several other monks if they knew anything about the feather.

Finally, one of the monks said, "That's the feather of faith—light, very light," as he laughed and blew the feather from the little monk's hands.

The little monk caught the feather before it hit the ground, held it in front of the candlelight and peered at the imprisoned splendor of colors he saw there in the peacock's tail. One should always look at the world through the feather of a peacock, the little monk decided.

Another brother came to the little monk for advice, but the little monk only listened.

27. When Every Day Is a Lenten Day

Winter would still not let go. The temperature dropped to its lowest. Six goats and four cows died that night. Before dawn that morning, Brother Kelpius went to get apples from the fruit cellar, but found none.

At chapter meeting later in the morning, Servant Jonathan seemed unusually forthright. "Some of you will not make it here in the monastic life," said the abbot by way of warning. "In this life, one never sees a letup to the required disciplines," Servant Jonathan continued.

"In *The Rule of St. Benedict* we hear these solemn words: 'A monk's life should always be like a Lenten observance.' Few there be who are capable of this."

Several of the monks gathered in chapter that day squirmed uneasily. Some knew in their hearts that they would not be able to run the full race.

"Many of you will enter the dark night of the soul and will find no light until you have left the monastery of Maloo. It is important that you enter the light wherever you can find it, whether here at Maloo, out in the world or in a place in the heart. Always remember, though, that the dark night of the soul, that point of seeming abandonment by God, is where God meets us and is most present to us. The dark night of the soul is the candle of the Lord. Do you recall what is written in Exodus about Moses? It says there:

'The people stood afar off, and Moses drew near to the thick darkness where God was.'

"Make no mistake. The soul was not made for perpetual Lent. Only when we realize that Easter always follows Lent, that Resurrection Easter follows Crucifixion Friday, can we stand the constant call to sacrificial living and dying. May this always be your attitude: if this be Lent, can Easter be far behind? However difficult your days here, there will come a time when you will walk in joy through these Lenten lands.

"To succeed here at Maloo, you must train your soul to seize the eucharistic moment at the heart of each hard day."

The monks shifted on the rough benches that held their bodies stiff. The little monk felt unsettled by this kind of talk. He pushed the words out of his mind as he focused on a spider crawling across his foot. A flicker of doubt stirred in his mind. He had given up all only to be told that some of the brothers might not make it to the end. He had come to the monastery expecting a course in miracles. Instead, he could see only the long, lengthening shadows of perpetual Lent. Some of the monks here would leave the monastery. He was sure of that. Is it I, Lord? he asked in his heart.

"The shadows of the monastery here at Maloo are the shadows of the cross of Christ. In coming to Maloo, you have come not to a dinner table but to a place of execution. Your soul will be crucified here. You will bear in your body and soul and mind and spirit the marks of the Lord Jesus," the abbot continued.

"You will recall that Benedict calls the monastery a school for God's service, a workshop for the soul. Maloo is not a finishing school for the religious, but an ending school for life as we know it. All you were and are will end here in the eternal practice of the *opus dei,* the work of worshiping

God through prayer, meditation and a life of praising God through the psalms.

"Nothing changes as slowly as a monastery. The eternal sameness of life here can eat your heart away," said the abbot. "Maloo is a gate into the potter's house where the Spirit shapes us in holiness." That awesome gate again, thought the little monk. The abbot forced the issue even more. "A life here barely succeeds except through the grace of God and the keeping of your vows. As you know, we ask of you, demand of you, three vows.

"First, you vow obedience to the gospel of Christ, to the monastic life, to the abbot and to the community.

"Second, you vow yourself to a search for ongoing conversion of life. If you ever give up on the ever-deepening conversion of your life into the life of Christ, there will be no place for you here at Maloo. There is only one way to succeed in this conversion of life, and that is through the encouraging, watchful ministry of the community of brothers here.

"Third, you take a vow of stability. This means that you give yourself to this community for life. You can only be a stabilizing force here if you plan on being here for the rest of your life. Thomas à Kempis, writer of *The Imitation of Christ*, spent fifty-two years in the same monastery. Only through the support of the community can one ever expect to fulfill such a vow. Nothing is more disastrous to the monastic life than monks on the move, switching from one monastery to another when things get hard or unpleasant."

The little monk looked at the face of the abbot to see any flicker of wavering on the seriousness of what was being said. But he saw only the cold reality of what it meant to become a monk for Christ's sake and not for one's own sake. The little monk's heart heard a hard truth, like the cold clang of a bell in winter.

The abbot closed his eyes. Silence fell over the room.

Some of the brothers groaned under the words of the abbot. Many breathed heavily, holding their arms around their chests and rocking back and forth. One by one they left the room to go to their cells and weigh their calling to Maloo.

As the little monk passed by the prayerful abbot, the abbot opened his eyes and spoke.

"Little monk, I need to discuss something with you. Please come to my office after Vespers today."

That afternoon, the little monk went to the riverbed to gather the last few stones for a labyrinth being built in the floor of the entrance to the chapel. When the labyrinth was finished, the monks would be able to walk the labyrinth daily as one of their spiritual disciplines.

As the little monk gathered stones in the frigid wind that day, he remembered the words often said by the abbot: "To those who believe, life is a labyrinth, not a maze."

The little monk used to think these two, labyrinth and maze, were the same until he came across a labyrinth in one of the cathedrals of France on his way to Maloo.

A priest at the cathedral explained the difference between a maze and a labyrinth to some eager pilgrims.

"In a maze, one hits dead ends. It is possible to lose oneself in the maze and never find the way out," explained the priest. "Such is often the way of the world.

"Though there seems to be many roads in a labyrinth, there really is only one road, taking the pilgrim ever closer and closer to the center of things. There are no dead ends or roadblocks. Only the ever-circling path to the center. As one gets closer to the center, there is an increase in spiritual depth and clarity. To those who believe, life is a labyrinth, not a maze!"

With joy did the little monk gather stones from the riverbed for such a project: a labyrinth in the floor of the cloister to the chapel at Maloo. His legacy would be this labyrinth, this tool of the soul's journey to God.

At the end of the day, after Vespers, the little monk appeared at the abbot's office. The little monk had not seen a foreshadowing of trouble, a turn of circumstance, a wrinkle in his status at the monastery.

"Little monk, we are concerned about you. While you have made great progress here, shared your wisdom with the common folk, been diligent in all the disciplines, we sense that there is a part of your life being held back from exposure to the light. Until all of your being is touched by the light, you cannot be a true monk of Maloo."

The words were swords to the heart.

The abbot sensed that the little monk still held back from the light some small area of his life. In the abbot's estimation, down under layer upon layer of promise, duty, devotion and surrender, lay one tiny speck of uncalculated self-deception. Yet, the little monk had no idea what that dark side of himself might be. What could be holding me back from becoming a brother to the Monk who rules the world, he wondered.

"But, there is something of greater concern," said the abbot, changing theme and mood. "There's trouble in the land, little monk. Trouble. Gorbon Kreeg has a stranglehold on the village and now has his fingers around the neck of the monastery, trying to bend it to his will.

"The village is being turned against us. Gorbon Kreeg has charmed the common folk and made enticing promises to the village officials. Many of the monks here are being influenced greatly by Gorbon Kreeg," continued the abbot. "There is a good possibility that a weaker monk may betray us."

I wonder who could ever do that, puzzled the little monk.

"But there's more. Gorbon Kreeg has brought accusations against you to the village council."

"What accusations?" asked the little monk, not used to having people make formal charges against him.

"Gorbon Kreeg accuses you of being too popular with the people and not having proper humility. He accuses you of insulting a judge in one of your dialogues. He accuses you of not being sincere. And he accuses you of an act of revolution."

"An act of revolution?" asked the little monk, surprised.

"Yes, he says that the journal you keep is an act of revolution. It allows you too many personal thoughts. It gives you a private life untouched and unmonitored by the rest of the monastic community, he says.

"His most serious charge is that you steal all kinds of small items, treasured things, that are precious to people," continued the abbot.

"Gorbon Kreeg is demanding that we place you on trial before the community. We have no other choice than to do that in the light of the power struggle going on here. The power seems to be his now. We want the truth to prevail. Perhaps an open trial is the best way for that to happen. We have to see this through. We must accommodate the enemy for the moment in order to win a victory later."

"I've never been to trial before," said the little monk, suddenly aware of a large burden on his shoulders.

"I hope you have good answers," added the abbot.

"So do I," mused the little monk.

In the face of these accusations, the little monk remained silent, except for asking one question: "What are you suggesting that I do?"

"Take some time off from the monastery. Live nearby so you can still breathe the holy air of Maloo. Do you know anyone you can stay with while you prepare for trial?"

"'I hope you have good answers,' added the abbot."

"No," replied the little monk, lost in thought.

"Then perhaps you should go home. Maybe you could return next year when things have settled down."

"No. I have a destiny here. Besides, I have no one at home either. My mother died some months ago, as you know. I have no other family." He wanted to say that he felt as if he were an orphan of two worlds and fitting into neither, but he held his peace.

"Well, think on these things," said the abbot. "In a week we will speak of them again. Meanwhile, I shall begin an investigation into the charges against you. Little monk, an idea just came to me. There is a man, a trustworthy friend of the monastery. He might be willing to take you in for a while. The people call him Old Immortality."

"Why do they call him that?" asked the little monk.

"Because he goes to the cemeteries of saints and martyrs. With hammer and chisel he cuts deeper the letters of their names."

"Why does he do that?" asked the little monk.

"'Lest ye forget,' is the only answer he ever offers," reported the abbot.

The little monk went to his cell. He remembered the first rule of a monk: "Go to your cell. It will teach you all things."

But today, his cell had nothing to teach him. No wisdom was there for him.

Purr was asleep. And so was the little monk's heart.

28. I'm Depressed!

*F*og—gray, heavy, wet, chilling, eerie—rolled across the grounds of the monastery. It came from the edge of a glacier caught in the claws of two rugged mountain peaks as the cool mountain air mixed itself with a warm backwind from the desert. This strange fog tumbled down the corridors of the monastery and slid under all the doors, filling the farthest corners of the monks' cells. Even in the dining hall the fog, like a cloud, hung close to the ceiling, while the monks shared a meal of cold potatoes, a crust of bread and some brown mixture that passed for gravy.

"Fog makes me depressed," said a brother monk.

"It always makes me just a little anxious," said another. "Why, I knew a villager who walked right off a cliff one time in the middle of a heavy fog. He must have felt he was near the edge of town. It was a month before they found his body." The little monk broke a crust of bread and dipped it in the gravy. His hand quickly lifted the sop to his hungry lips and then he licked his fingers.

"Fog makes me feel scared and alone," said yet another brother. "It shuts out vision. It hides and distorts everything. Anything, absolutely anything, could happen in this kind of dense fog. It sneaks up on you and throws a pall-gray net over you. It cuts off the world."

The little monk, though, liked the fog. When he was very young, his family lived in a foggy highland region. He had grown up with a morning fog throughout most of the winter season. To him, the fog covered everything with a soft, quiet peace. "Peace is at the center of the fog. A good fog always reminds me of the mood of contemplation," said the little monk.

That afternoon, the monks went in search of nettles for making St. Benedict's soup. The monastery at Maloo, by custom, tried to make this soup four times a year, if the seasons allowed. They had to wear gloves to gather the nettles in order not to be pricked or stung. They found a few nettles hidden in the rocks and somewhat protected from the winter blasts.

"In spite of their prickly leaves, nettles do make a tasty soup," the abbot had told them.

When the monks returned from gathering the few available nettles, they picked up the discussion of feeling depressed.

"All I know is don't allow yourself to get too depressed or you'll find a sign on your cell door from the abbot," said one of the monks.

"What kind of sign?" asked another.

"One word—*acedia.*"

"What does that mean?"

"It means 'sloth,' one of the seven deadly sins," answered the brother monk.

Another monk named these sins on his fingers: "Pride, sloth, envy, anger, avarice, gluttony, and lust."

"Let's ask the novice master about this later in our meeting with him," suggested one of the monks.

"Sloth will make a good topic for us today," said Brother Stephen later. "Usually the issue comes up sooner, after a few signs have appeared on doors," the novice master said, taking up the challenge.

"The seven deadly sins are prickly things. They have the sting of death to them. Of the seven, one that is most likely to work its way into the lives of monks like us is sloth, or acedia."

"We were discussing this. What is this *acedia* or *sloth*? We're confused," one of the brothers offered.

"*Acedia* can be any one of a long list of things: despair, melancholy, listlessness, boredom, apathy, ongoing sadness without relief, idleness, desirelessness, sluggishness, no energy or sense of life, being morbid or cast down, or just experiencing an increasing slack in spiritual things. These can all be summed up in the words 'spiritual depression,'" explained the novice master.

"In other words," continued Brother Stephen, "we are held accountable for this spiritual depression."

"You're not talking about all kinds of depression, are you?" asked a concerned brother.

"No," replied the novice master, "those who work in the cure of souls have always been careful to distinguish between three kinds of depression—depression due to some kind of chemical imbalance not under the person's control; a temporary trauma depression brought on by some tragedy of sorts; and spiritual depression brought on by Satan's attack or general spiritual malaise or indifference.

"It is this last kind of spiritual apathy that David, the psalmist, dealt with when he declared, 'I will lift up my soul.' David took responsibility for the health of his soul. One can allow spiritual despair to overcome the soul or one can fight it off with the resources of the Holy Spirit."

"So, we are held accountable for resisting each of these seven deadly sins?" queried a monk.

"Yes, and that includes acedia, or sloth," answered Brother Stephen, pleased that they were grasping the principles involved. "If you want to know what hell is like, it is made of endless boredom and sloth. St. Thomas Aquinas defined *acedia* as sadness in the face of spiritual good. It is

"The abbot hung the same ugly sign on his own door."

the refusal of joy. It is despair of the mercy of God. When caught up in acedia, we refuse to be comforted by God and doubt his very mercy and reject his joy.

"So, even be careful that a dull, gray day doesn't begin to pull you down into the pit of sloth," concluded Brother Stephen.

Fighting sloth, defeating acedia, will be a hard thing for us monks to learn, thought the little monk.

Like an endless cobweb, the rainy mist hung from the sky all that day and evening.

In spite of the good instruction that day, during the middle of the night, the abbot hung an ugly green sign "ACEDIA" on a monk's door across the hall from the little monk's cell.

The lesson had begun.

A few nights later, the abbot hung the same ugly sign on his own door. Even the abbot had to continue to do battle with this deadly sin.

29. A Pilgrim's Progress

*T*he little monk received his work assignment for the day. "Someone needs to scrub the labyrinth floor in front of the chapel," said the abbot, looking at the little monk.

The little monk picked up his bucket and a few rags and headed toward the chapel.

He stopped to survey again the meaning of the labyrinth. He put his hand over his eyes to shield them from the brilliant sunlight pouring in from one of the cloister windows. Someone had told him once that the idea of labyrinth had developed as a substitute for a real pilgrimage to Jerusalem.

He stepped onto the labyrinth he himself had helped build by carrying stones from the riverbed. He walked the long narrow lines of stone, circling ever inward to the center. To arrive at the center is to find heavenly Jerusalem, the center of all things, the home of God.

Then he knelt down and began to scrub clean the labyrinth floor so that it would be ready for the next pilgrim who might come along.

As he worked, his mind floated on a cloud of fine memories. He remembered how his mother used to take him aside and read to him, everything from the Bible to stories about the martyrs and saints, from history to great literature.

One of his favorite stories, he remembered, had been John Bunyan's *Pilgrim's Progress*. He marveled even now how a person could weave into one story all of the seven deadly sins as well as many of the great Christian virtues.

"One time his mother took him to a London church that had a set of stained-glass windows depicting scenes from Pilgrim's Progress."

Some of the images came easily back to mind: characters such as Mr. Love-lust, Gripe-man and Sir Having Greedy; of cities such as Apostasy, Destruction and Fair-speech; of biblical symbols such as Immanuel's land, the Shining Ones (angels) and House Beautiful; of such places as By-path Meadow, the Delectable Mountains, Doubting Castle, Difficulty Hill and the Slough of Despond; and of a weapon called "all-prayer."

One time his mother took him to a London church that had a set of stained-glass windows depicting scenes from *Pilgrim's Progress.* For hours on end he stood with his mother, peering at the windows as sunlight spilling through turned the windows into living color. He never forgot that experience. He often dated the beginning of his longing for God to the sight of those windows.

These grand images from his memory began to lay themselves over the labyrinth floor until the pilgrim images and the labyrinth mysteries became one.

His mind and heart filled to overflowing with felicity, that greatest of human emotions. Servant Jonathan once defined *felicity* as complete joy, the highest of joy.

The little monk began to hum a part of his song, "The Little Monk's Song." He came to the words about dropping his pilgrim bag by the side of the road. He thought again of the pilgrim in Bunyan's story and how this pilgrim arrived in Jerusalem and, coming to Calvary, stood at the foot of the cross of Christ. His pilgrim's bag fell off his back and to the ground, where it rolled down a hill and into the resurrection tomb, never to be seen again.

Now, that's the truth, the little monk said to himself, slapping his knee. He scrubbed his way to the very center of the labyrinth and stayed there on his knees, praying without ceasing.

He did not notice a family who had come to visit the monastery. The young boy pointed to the little monk praying and said to his mother and father, "There's a pilgrim. When I grow up, I want to be a pilgrim, too."

The abbot, Servant Jonathan, saw this scene from afar and said to the little monk, "Go scrub the crosses in the cemetery. The pilgrims who sleep there need your attention."

As he scrubbed the crosses and the stone crevices where the dead had their names chiseled, he thought of the holy bones beneath the ground and how the oldest grave always becomes the home for the newest occupant. When a monk dies, the oldest grave in the cemetery is opened and the bones of that old saint are gathered up into a small pile at one end of the grave to form the pillow for the next pilgrim to sleep on in the dust of the ground.

Someday, I too will become the pillow for the next pilgrim, the little monk pondered.

"Each pilgrim," he remembered Servant Jonathan saying, "rests upon the other until we all finally lay our heads on the bosom of Christ."

The little monk prayed aloud, "O God, take the dimness of my soul away."

Then he turned to scrub another cross.

30. Journey to the Seventh Gift

T he time came for the little monk to leave the monastery for a while to confront himself and to await the outcome of the accusations that Gorbon Kreeg brought against him.

He left without being able to speak to anyone except the abbot, Servant Jonathan.

"Go in peace, little monk," said the abbot. "Our prayers are with you. May you expose all of your life to the light—even the hidden parts. In the meantime we will make final plans for the trial and how best to answer Gorbon Kreeg. Prepare well, little monk. I think he means to trick you."

The little monk picked up Purr on his way out. She sensed that something was amiss when he put her in the flour sack he carried her in whenever they went on a journey.

"Do you know where Old Immortality lives?" the little monk asked cautiously, when he arrived at the village.

"No. I've only seen him at a distance. Never talked to him. I wouldn't trust him if I were you," said one villager, giving a warning.

"Why?"

"Well, there's just something about him that's suspicious. Not that he's ever robbed anyone or anything like that. He's just mysterious, you know. A little odd."

The little monk asked several villagers how he could find Old Immortality. None could point the way. "I heard that he lives near the desert's edge," said one. "I think he lives on the mountain somewhere," said another. "I think he lives beyond the meadow," replied a third. "In the forest. Yes, in the forest, I think," a merchant told him.

"There aren't too many roads around Maloo. Probably any road you take will go by his house," the village philosopher told him.

Finally one person told him: "Ask the children. The children know. The children know most of what goes on in Maloo."

The little monk decided to do just that. He located a small group of children playing and splashing in the village fountain near the market square. Before asking his question, he knew it was important to join them in their play. He slipped off his sandals and stepped into the fountain. The children baptized him with huge splashes of water. They took him captive and held him under the spray that came out of the top of the fountain and then fell over the sides of a huge stone urn. His robe floated on the surface of the water, making him look big and fat. The children laughed and called him a whale. The winter was past.

Later, as they sat on the fountain's edge, drying off, he asked them "Do you know where Old Immortality lives?"

"Sure," the children said.

"He lives near my house," said a lad with no shoes. "Just beyond Prophets' Point. I'll show you. Follow me," he said, taking off at a brisk pace up the gravel path toward the forest. The bottoms of his feet were as tough as shoe leather.

Blessed are the feet, thought the little monk, that bring good tidings. The little monk kept off his sandals and went barefoot, like the lad who led him.

The journey took them down what the local people called the King's Highway. Even though it was only a path, the king of that land had once walked along it.

"His robe floated on the surface of the water, making him look big and fat."

"There's the house," the boy said, pointing at a very plain-looking cottage of weathered gray stone and small, high windows. The forest grew thickly right up to the house. Some passersby might not even see the house, so hidden was it.

He turned to thank the child who had led him to the house, but the boy had already disappeared into the dense woods.

A small curl of smoke rose like incense from the chimney of the house.

The little monk found the gate hard to open. It seemed to have not been used much. Looks like not many visitors ever come this way, he thought. The latch on the gate was rusting and the hinges seemed stuck. But, he finally pushed open the old gate.

The little monk knocked at the door to the cottage. Silence. He knocked again. Silence. He knocked a third time and the door opened to a scene of remarkable surprise. There stood the shepherd, the one the little monk had encountered several times before.

"Welcome," said the shepherd. "My home is your home."

The whole house smelled of goodness and trust. Flowers decked out each room. Books were all around. Plain and simple beauty filled the room. The whole place was a prayer for the eye.

What a glorious place this is, thought the little monk. It's like an enchanted cottage, he decided. Then he remembered a story of an enchanted cottage. An ugly woman had worked for years in the city. The city was no friend to her ugliness. She met rejection on every hand at social gatherings. One day she had saved enough money to buy a small house far removed from people. She lived in peace, but also in loneliness. One day a woodcutter knocked on her door looking for work, chopping wood. After his chopping, he knocked at the door again to receive his pay. "I can pay you in full or partly with dinner," she offered. "Dinner would be fine," he answered. She showed him where to wash up.

They had a grand dinner that night, in spite of her ugliness, and had many more grand dinners for months thereafter. One day this handsome man remarked about her beauty. She beamed in satisfaction. But later, she remembered the former owner telling her a legend about this cottage—one can only see beauty here, never ugliness.

During the next dinner, he asked for her hand in marriage. But she refused and gave no reason. He continued to ask for an explanation, but she would give none. Finally, she told him that this was an enchanted cottage and that he had no choice but to tell her that she was beautiful, when all the world knew how ugly she was.

"This is a strange place where illusions and reality meet," the handsome man answered. "Don't you know that I'm ugly, too, and that in this enchanted cottage, you have no choice but to see me as handsome. So then, we are both either beautiful or ugly, but does it matter which, if we love each other? The true story of this enchanted cottage is that love has its own beauty."

This shepherd's house is an enchanted cottage, too—concluded the little monk. He wondered what he would find here—illusion or reality.

After a dinner fit for a king, the shepherd and the little monk retired to the living room to talk.

"You know why I'm here, don't you?" asked the little monk. "Gorbon Kreeg has brought many accusations against me, stirred up the monastery in controversy and the abbot has asked me to leave the monastery for a while. I'm to stand trial in the village. I had no other place to go, no one else to turn to. All I want is to be a good monk."

"Gorbon Kreeg is a wild and dangerous man. He roams the earth lusting for power and recognition," said the shepherd. "But like all men of his kind, he has a tragic flaw. His ambition has within it the seeds of his own destruction."

"Why can't people like him learn to seek simplicity?" asked the little monk.

"Because simplicity is a gift from God," replied the shepherd.

"I pray for Gorbon Kreeg," the little monk said softly.

"You've chosen the royal road then. True prayer dispels all illusion," replied the shepherd. Then he changed the subject: "So, you've finally come for the gift?"

Not knowing where all this was going to lead, the little monk answered, "Yes."

"What is the gift?" asked the little monk.

"It's really the seventh gift," replied the shepherd.

The seventh gift? Where have I heard that before? thought the little monk. Then he remembered the abbot's story about the princess and the seventh gift. And he also remembered that the abbot said that a shepherd told him the story. This man now before me is that shepherd, concluded the little monk.

"You're the shepherd who gave the abbot the story of the seventh gift," declared the little monk.

"What is important is whether you find your own seventh gift," said the shepherd. "I promise to help all I can."

"I need to find the other six gifts first," replied the little monk.

"You already have those," answered the shepherd. "Your mother gave you love; your bishop gave you a dream; your cat, Purr, has given you unconditional friendship; Maloo has given you the gift of unceasing prayer; God has given you a way of wisdom that the common people can understand— a view of things as simple as a grain of wheat; and I gave you a hazelnut for hope. There, you have it, six gifts. The seventh gift may be harder to come by. But God will give the gift when you're most ready. The seventh gift is given only to those who listen deeply. We all need a seventh gift to make us whole."

"What could that gift be for me?" asked the little monk.

"The seventh gift is that which God provides in our lowest moments," said the shepherd.

"But I may never discover what my seventh gift is," the little monk said rather forlornly. "The only gift I really want is to be a monk of Maloo. A monk of Maloo can change the world."

"Now is the time for a great dealing of God in the interior castle of your soul," said the shepherd. "Sometimes the soul erects signposts reading, 'no trespassing,'" instructed the shepherd, writing the words in the air with his finger.

"In this inner kingdom, there are often uncharted regions, wilderness places hidden from the light, places where God is forbidden to go. This is that part of the soul where we refuse to let the sovereignty of God reign. This is that part of us we have never accepted and cannot let God love. This is the land of desolation. The deepest conviction we have is that if God saw this part of us, he would no longer love us."

The little monk sighed because of the burden he carried. He felt wearied by the load of his pilgrim's bag. The shepherd never seems to tire, the little monk thought to himself. He recalled Servant Jonathan's insight: "Old saints walk more lightly upon earth's globe. Their shoes never wear out, for these old saints walk a path just a little above the earth."

"Sometimes we have done such a complete job of hiding the vulnerable part of us that we can no longer find that secret place ourselves. We've misplaced the key to this locked door."

"How will the door ever be opened, then?" asked the little monk, sadness filling his eyes.

"The key is right where you left it," said the shepherd mysteriously.

The little monk nodded as if he knew what the shepherd was talking about.

"Let me take you to your room," said the shepherd, leading the way. "Before I do, let me remind you that Jesus himself had seven gifts within him. In his prophecy about Christ, Isaiah wrote that the Messiah would come endowed with seven gifts: wisdom, understanding, counsel, strength, knowledge, the fear of the Lord and the spirit of discernment. If our Lord, in his humanity, needed seven gifts, how much more the sons and daughters of the Lord?"

The shepherd put a hand on the little monk's shoulder as the two looked at each other. Then the shepherd touched the little monk's heart with his finger. "The answer is here," he said, pointing to the little monk's heart. The little monk looked down at his heart and offered a brief prayer.

The time of words was ended.

The shepherd left. The door closed. Alone with the Alone.

31. The Candle of the Lord in a Dark Room

*T*he room lay in darkness, except for a slit of moonlight slipping between the two edges of the curtains hanging across the small window.

He lighted a candle resting on the table.

The little monk thought that the room looked no larger than his monk's cell and seemed just as meager: a rough bed, a crude table and an aged washstand. Yet, an unusual warmth held the scene together, like a memory softened by time. Just like home, the little monk thought, referring to the rugged simplicity of things around him at Maloo.

The silence that comes with sacred moments, those pivotal times in the private spaces of the soul, filled the room. Every corner of it.

His thoughts turned again to his problems. I don't know what it is that I'm holding back and what I need as a seventh gift, he mumbled to himself.

"Always pray from the deepest well," his mother taught him. Until I can surrender to God all of myself, I will never know what the deepest well is, thought the little monk, as he sighed again.

He sat down in a hard-backed chair and said Compline, the night prayer to be offered before one retires. He closed Compline with this collect: Keep watch, dear Lord, with those who work, or watch or weep this night, and give your angels charge over those who sleep. Tend the sick, Lord

Christ; give rest to the weary, bless the dying, soothe the suffering, pity the afflicted, shield the joyous; and all in your love's sake.

He sat for a long time, gazing into empty space, until the candle on the table almost went out before he realized that he needed to light a new candle. The other one had burned itself down to a pile of wick and wax.

On the other side of midnight, the little monk turned to his first love—finding Christ in the scriptures. He opened his Bible on his lap, and, as was the ancient tradition of monasteries, he read aloud. He read passionately and thoughtfully into the early hours of the morning. He read the scriptures into the depths of his soul. The thing is to become soaked with the word of God, he concluded. He wanted the last hidden corner of his soul to be fully converted. One of the three great vows of the monastery at Maloo was a commitment to ongoing conversion. What better tool to convert the soul than the word of God, he concluded.

In his reading of the gospel, he came to this passage in John: "You search the scriptures, because you think that in them you have eternal life; and it is they that bear witness to me; yet you refuse to come to me."

The little monk read and meditated all night, searching for that which would speak perfectly and completely to his condition. Near to exhaustion now and wearied by his inner turmoil, he prayed, "O God, something in me there is that fights off your sovereignty. Show me what it is."

As the darkness of night turned to twilight gray, the little monk's thoughts about himself faded and turned to thoughts of Christ. He wondered if Christ in his humanity ever had anything of a dark side to himself.

He shook off this thought as if it smacked of heresy. But the harder he tried to shake it off the more intrigued he was by the idea. If there was anything that bothered Christ, I wonder what it was, thought the little monk. A sudden insight pierced his mind, like a toothache in its first shooting pain: Christ never really fit in, did he? Christ was always out of step with the world around him. Even those who believed sometimes forsook him. His mother, father and disciples had trouble understanding him. How sad to never really be accepted or understood by anyone. Of all the things that Christ faced, never fitting in with people must have given a sad edge to his life.

"And to yours," a soundless voice said. This truth struck the little monk to the core of his being.

Days passed into weeks, while the little monk continued to live in the shepherd's house. No final, clear answers came. Only a notion of impending purpose. Why am I falsely accused? How can God benefit by my expulsion from the monastery? I've tried so hard; how could something like this happen to me? How can I deal with my dark side that resists the light of God? Nothing but questions.

He thought of something Servant Jonathan once told the novices: "Always remember, the dark night of the soul is the candle of the Lord."

One afternoon, the little monk studied a bright painting on the wall of his room. He went closer to examine it. The painting showed a young lad fishing on a glorious summer day. The painting was steeped in joyful colors. He started to move away from the painting but saw something that startled him. A slingshot hung out of the lad's back pocket. At a distance away, beneath some underbrush, lay a dead squirrel and beside its bleeding head a rough stone, obviously flung from the lad's slingshot.

Now it all came back to the little monk, the nightmare, the evil he had always hidden from himself. When the little monk was a small boy, he had tried to fit in with the other boys. One day they took their slingshots out to the woods to shoot at birds on the wing. Stones flew every which way from a dozen slingshots. None connected except his. He hit a bird directly in the head and wing. It fluttered out of control and fell dead at their feet. The other boys cheered and crowned him a hero. Later that evening he came back sadly to look at the dead body of the bird. Horror filled his veins. He buried the evidence in the ground—and in his heart. He never told anyone about his deed, certainly never to brag about it.

This was his first act of conscious evil. It lingered within him, often spilling out in dreams and unguarded moments of reflection. This act was all the evidence heaven needed that he was a sinner, he thought.

How criminal, how evil this act of violence. This was the decay at the bottom of his soul that held him back from complete surrender to God. This was the rust on the hinge that kept him from swinging wide the gate to his heart so God could come in, a guest welcome in all parts of the house. How could God ever love anyone who deliberately killed such an innocent part of God's creation? he wondered. He had shed innocent blood. Though it was only the blood of a bird, still it was innocent blood. It always made him feel that he had a direct hand in the shedding of Christ's blood.

He had never known how to deal with such evil buried so deep within his fundamental makeup as a person. Who can deliver me? he wondered. All his life he had been unforgiven, at least by himself.

In the shepherd's cottage now, he remembered the sling he had tied to his waist. He took it out and put it on the table. It represented the darkness within him. He carried it to the fireplace, prayed for forgiveness and seemed ready to toss it into the burning flames. But, he remembered the counsel given to him when he first came to Maloo and offered his sling to the leaders: "Tie that sling to your waist and if you ever see the Devil, fling three stones at him—one for Adam, one Eve, and one for Jesus." He tied the sling tightly to his waist again.

Later in the day, he sat on the porch of the shepherd's house, rocking in a chair. Purr slept curled up in his lap. The little monk realized that the shepherd had been showering him with gifts all along: a piece of jade, a flute, a feather, a clove of garlic, a hazelnut, as well as these most recent acts of hospitality and nurture. All had come from him. Then the little monk leaned his head against the back of the chair to let his mind roam freely. The sun warmed his face. He rocked and rocked and rocked.

Like an autumn leaf falling slowly onto one's shoulder, so did a simple thought land on the edge of his mind and startled him. "You are loved. What other meaning could you possibly need? Let go of worrying about your dark side. Let go of Maloo. Let go of needing to be understood. Let go of trying to figure out the patterns of life, why this happens or that. Let go of the murdered bird. Let go of the dark side of the self. Love is the only meaning you need. And you are loved."

The significance of such love overwhelmed this little man who sat in a rocking chair, in the sun, with a cat in the lap, on the shepherd's porch, deep in the forest, not far from Prophets' Point, down a path called the King's Highway, on an ordinary day in the year of our Lord when God kept his promises and loosed his love again.

God's love is all that matters, the little monk decided. The love of God is the father of all meaning. Love is his meaning, as Julian of Norwich affirms.

The little monk lingered in contemplation for quite some time and then turned in his journal to words of the poet Hopkins, who wrote of "the utter freshness of deep down things."

"A messenger came on a dark horse."

But just as soon as love showed up, fear—fear of the future—also made its customary visit. What will I say at my trial? wondered the little monk. There had been no word from God yet on how to proceed at the trial.

He sat on the porch listening and waiting, but there was no wind that day.

Suddenly, a messenger came on a dark horse. "The trial is set. Tomorrow afternoon at four o'clock," he yelled before riding on to herald the news throughout the woods and valley. Hearing the noise, the shepherd came out on the porch to receive the news.

"It's time," said the little monk. "The waiting is over. Will you sit at the trial with me, shepherd?"

"I wouldn't be a friend if I didn't. Now, go quickly. I'll join you by trial time. Perhaps this trial will give us the opportunity to seize the eucharistic moment when God will act. Go on ahead. I will follow soon."

On his way back to Maloo, the little monk sang the song he had written for himself.

"Purr," he said, "do you remember what Hildegard of Bingen said? 'The Devil has no song to sing,' she said. Isn't that sad, Purr? Only those who are forgiven by God have a song to sing.

"Sing, Purr, sing."

A sparrow flew overhead in the unhindered sky.

32. In the Courtroom of Gorbon Kreeg

The next day at the appointed time, the little monk stopped at the gate to the village hall. He carried Purr in her traveling sack. When the little monk put his hand to the gate to open it, a mean dog with scabs and scars, dirty fur, yellow teeth and a cropped tail from a long-ago battle growled fiercely at him. But he pushed on through the gate. The dog backed down and whimpered away when the little monk stared him down with a look that said, "I'm here on kingdom business."

"I bet they find the little monk guilty," a villager whispered to his friend as the little monk entered the village hall.

The hall was crowded with scores of people for this village-wide event. Most of the town officials sat with Gorbon Kreeg at a large, heavy table to one side of the room. At Gorbon Kreeg's right hand sat a monk of Maloo— the monk who had been teaching heresy, the one who had been ignoring his spiritual director, the one who had sought out the little monk's advice, the one who had shown repentance.

The abbot and the shepherd sat alone at a smaller table. Surprised that the shepherd was already there, the little monk moved to the table. People strained to see the accused, looking him up and down to make from that survey their first judgment as to whether he was guilty or not. To most, he looked guilty.

"A mean dog growled fiercely at him…"

The little monk had brought Purr along, but Gorbon Kreeg insisted that she not be allowed to stay. The mayor of the village served as judge for the proceedings.

"Purr cannot stay," he decided. "Someone take her outside."

The little monk rubbed the back of her ears and handed her to one of the town officials, who carried her by the nape of her neck, her body hanging limply. But one of the children rescued her and carried her outside, consoling her the whole time.

Before the trial began, Gorbon Kreeg approached the little monk's table.

"I feel sorry for you, little monk. Don't you know that the world is ruled by personalities, not principles? One can change the course of history by the sheer force of personality. Think of all the personalities who shaped history to their liking. No one follows just a leader. Everyone follows a strong personality. I'm a personality, little monk, a personality. By the strength of my personality, the village is mine. Soon, the monastery will be mine. You could be a personality, too, little monk. You've the makings for that. You're already somewhat of a legend. If you would only leave this abbot and shepherd behind and follow me, I could give you a kingdom."

The little monk started to say something, but then remembered the shepherd's advice: "Keep yourself in silence. One who is kept in silence is held safely in the arms of God."

Faced only with silence, Gorbon Kreeg shrugged his shoulders and shook his head in disbelief.

The hours wore on and the trial marched toward dusk. The accusations were many and various "witnesses" added their own comments.

"I've seen him write down all sorts of things in that book of his," said a villager, pointing to the journal lying closed on the little monk's table.

"He can't be too holy," said another witness, "if he's always doing things outside of the monastery. He should be cloistered and not allowed to roam about."

"He spends too much time with that silly cat and not enough on serious, holy things."

"He crawls into his robe and ignores people."

"He insults our leaders and shows them up in front of the common people."

"He begs food from people who have little for themselves."

The villagers all seemed to have turned against the little monk. The disease of rumor, lies, half-truths and gossip spread throughout the room, infecting each succeeding witness.

Then the monk of Maloo who had defected to Gorbon Kreeg's side reported, "The little monk deceives us all. He makes a show of holiness, but he's not a true monk of Maloo. The abbot has had to reprimand him several times." He looked at the abbot, who certainly would have to concur with this last statement. The abbot frowned in disbelief.

"The little monk steals," the corrupted monk declared. "His room is full of things he has taken from others—a vase, a beautiful peacock's feather, a flute and many other cherished items." If this last charge was found to be true, the crowd knew the little monk would be declared guilty.

Gorbon Kreeg leaned over and whispered to several of his disciples. A short round of mocking laughter ensued.

So this is what it was like for Christ to face the mob, thought the abbot.

The wolves have tasted the blood of the lamb, the shepherd noted to himself.

This is the door to an awful darkness, concluded the little monk.

A sinister smile crept across Gorbon Kreeg's face as he considered the picture before him: an abbot, a shepherd and a little monk, none of whom had any real power.

The little monk touched the sling tied to his waist.

Gorbon Kreeg's process in the trial was to give an overview of accusations, then bear down hard on each one with considerable evidence and witnesses. Gorbon Kreeg was a master prosecutor and built his case with infinite patience. If he could destroy the little monk's reputation, the village and the monastery would be his. These would be just stepping-stones to taking the next village and the next until he had captured a kingdom.

But, when they got to this part of the trial, the shepherd leaned over and whispered to the little monk, "No matter what the accusation, just hold up a hazelnut and tell them that Jesus is Lord."

The little monk turned in his chair to survey the shepherd's face to see if he was serious. He was. The little monk was more than puzzled by this word from the shepherd. The little monk looked at the abbot for confirmation. The abbot smiled knowingly and nodded. The little monk was still unsure of the counsel given to him by the shepherd. Then, he heard a voice within himself say, "This is the seventh gift." The little monk knew that the Promiser of all things was in this eucharistic moment, that the shepherd of Maloo had bestowed a good gift.

"Stand, little monk, and hear these accusations against you," said the mayor.

The little monk stood alone in the center of the room.

When each accusation had been fully developed, the mayor would ask, "What say, ye, little monk, to this accusation?"

On the first accusation, the little monk stood for a long time in silence. Finally, the mayor said loudly, "What say, ye, little monk, to this accusation?"

The little monk looked back at the shepherd who only nodded. Then he looked at the abbot, who sat with his eyes closed and his hands folded in his lap, obviously in prayer. Out of the corner of his eye, the little monk saw a spider on the floor. He nudged it aside gently with his foot. The little monk turned again and looked deeply into the eyes of his accusers, then into Gorbon Kreeg's cold, calculating eyes.

The little monk reached into his pocket, pulled out a hazelnut and held it high for all to see. Then he witnessed to a great truth, "Jesus is Lord."

The courtroom fell quiet. "Is that all you have to say?" asked the mayor. But the little monk remained silent. They went on to the next accusation and its evidence. "What say ye, little monk, to this accusation?" asked the mayor. The little monk held up the hazelnut again and declared, "Jesus is Lord."

Rage swallowed up Gorbon Kreeg and spread to his disciples. Gorbon Kreeg tried to sputter his protest at this turn in the case. But the mayor raised his hand. "Is Jesus Lord or not, Gorbon Kreeg?" asked the mayor. Gorbon Kreeg thought it best to remain silent.

Accusation after accusation against the little monk was answered by the simple show of a hazelnut and a heralding of, "Jesus is Lord."

Halfway through the accusations, the little monk thrust the hazelnut high above his head and one by one the common people began to pick up the chant of victory, "Jesus is Lord." By the end of the accusations the crowd was on its feet shouting and many reached out to touch this common hazelnut as if it were a sacred relic.

Outside, stirred by the shouts, Purr jumped up on the window ledge. In the dusk, by the growing light of the moon, Purr's head cast an odd shadow across the figure of Gorbon Kreeg that transformed his visage into that of a

*"An odd shadow…transformed his visage
into that of a boar's head."*

boar's head. Several people shivered in fright when they saw such a shadow. Gorbon Kreeg's eyes narrowed into two flat slits of red rage.

The people began to dance around the little monk. Gorbon Kreeg pushed his way through the crowd to the little monk. Just inches from the little monk's face, Gorbon Kreeg hissed the vilest of warnings. "I take an oath today, little monk, that until the day I die I will seek every means to destroy you. Even if it takes selling my soul to the Devil, I will pay you back for this, little monk. May God take my life, if I don't make yours a hell."

The little monk touched Gorbon Kreeg's arm gently, and said, "Gorbon Kreeg, do you not know that the road to Calvary has a narrow gate?"

Then Gorbon Kreeg jerked his arm away, knocking the hazelnut to the floor. He stomped on it, smashing it into hundreds of tiny pieces. The people gasped, but then shouted down Gorbon Kreeg with, "Jesus is Lord."

Gorbon Kreeg moved toward the door, winced a little, unaware that a piece of hazelnut shell had cut his foot. After cursing the whole village, he and his disciples stormed out of the room.

The little monk looked at the abbot and knew that the monastery was saved. Then he looked back at the shepherd, who simply raised aloft his old rugged staff.

The mood grew so triumphant in the hall that the occasion quickly turned into a celebration. The villagers brought food and drink in abundance for everyone, with music, laughter and dance following.

Not forgetting Purr, the little monk dipped his finger into a large bowl of plum pudding and held it for Purr to lick.

"Purr, the kingdom of God is a banquet—a real party, Purr," he said, breaking off a piece of mince pie and giving Purr a generous taste.

33. The Calvary Road Has a Narrow Gate

*T*he trial took a lot out of the little monk. The abbot sent him on retreat to a desert cave for forty days and nights, the time Jesus himself had been in the wilderness. While Purr explored the cave, the little monk had little there but a thorn-bush on which he meditated from time to time and an old raven who watched him. And the wind—always the wind.

"There life slows down to the pace of eternity," he would tell others when they asked about his desert experience. "The sun burns out the last ounce of resistance or pride," he would tell them. "Out there in the desert, I lose the hurry inside of me. Then the Holy Spirit begins his work. No wonder the desert fathers often cried aloud, 'Flee to the desert. Flee to the desert!' They knew how perfectly the boredom, sameness, endlessness of the desert sets in motion the pure work of the cross. There is no pride left in the desert. There is only a firm grasp of the cross."

"What do you do in the desert?" inquirers would ask. "I pray without ceasing," the little monk usually would reply. "I read through the entire Bible in my wilderness experience there. I sing and praise and pray. There is so little time, you know, when one is doing real soul-work at the cross."

When the little monk returned this time to the monastery at Maloo, they informed him that a guest was waiting to see him. He greeted her warmly in the spirit of St. Benedict's

*"The little monk had little there but a thornbush...
and an old raven."*

counsel: "All guests who present themselves at the monastery are to be welcomed as Christ."

She was a member of a king's court and wanted spiritual counsel. This king's domain was far away. She was a woman of great prominence and notoriety. She was interested in providing a spiritually guided leadership, but the trappings of her wealth often got in the way. After greeting her, the little monk took her to the garden, where they sat on the stone bench under the copper beech trees near the garden gate.

"Please help me, little monk," she said. "I'm having difficulty breaking through to God in a final, ultimate way. I have some spiritual perception, but need so much help to break through to God. I've been too long in the dark cloud of unknowing. There is nothing but the dark night of the soul. You're known throughout the region for teaching the simplicity of prayer."

This moved the little monk to compassion. "You may feel that you are in darkness, but I see light all around you. Jesus said, 'Whoever follows me shall not walk in darkness.' Thomas à Kempis commented about that in this way, 'These are the words of Christ, whereby we are admonished how we must imitate his life and conversation if we would be truly enlightened and delivered from all blindness of the heart. Let it, then, be our chief study to meditate on the life of Jesus Christ.' Then he went on to add: 'It is no small thing to gain or lose the kingdom of God.'"

"But how may I live in imitation of Christ, when my sins weigh me down so?" asked the woman, removing her expensive cloak in order to be more comfortable.

"You will begin to imitate Christ when you love him more than anything else in the world," the little monk offered. "While in the desert I read again with great solace the *Spiritual Letters* of Fénelon. Brother Fénelon said: 'Love him, and I will release you of every other obligation. For everything else will come by love. All I ask is that your will should lean toward love.'"

"Beyond loving him with all my heart, what else must I do to imitate my Lord?" the woman asked, moved by the words of the little monk, words she desperately wanted to hear. The little monk proceeded cautiously. He wanted to be sure that this woman was ready for the full message of the cross. He knew how terrible it was for a soul to come under the shadow of the cross, and then to draw back and retreat into despair.

"Love and obedience go hand in hand," the little monk announced. "Fénelon declared, 'The only principle you need to be concerned about is to be scrupulously obedient.' You must obey the call of the cross without reservation. The cross will humble you until the only thing you ever want is to disappear into the cross of Christ and never be found again.'

"Let me add only this: The gate is narrow on this road least traveled. St. Benedict urged, 'Do not be daunted immediately by fear and run away from the road that leads to salvation. It is bound to be narrow at the outset.'"

"But that's so hard for me," the woman replied. "I'm a person of prominence. I'm talented. God has given me great gifts for leading people and speaking to groups. All over my country invitations come to speak to various groups about modern spirituality. Lately, I've begun to feel like I have to impress them, to perform better each and every time, to give them something different to grow on, to excite them with great new truths."

"All those who serve God, sooner or later, have gone down that road, thinking that everything depends on them, on their ability to dazzle people. There is nothing appealing at all to the flesh in the final crucifixion of the soul," responded the little monk.

"We have to learn to love personal obscurity and to leave the world to entertain itself," continued the little monk. "Many want to hear of things more dazzling and sensational than the 'Good News.' There is nothing more than the 'Good News.' That's all we everyday monks have to offer. Plain and simple. The gospel is as old as bread and wine and as new and fresh as a birth announcement."

"What else do I need in order to enter into the imitation of Christ?" the woman questioned, ready to make a complete commitment, holding nothing back. "Should I sell all that I have and give to the poor?"

"Who, then, would minister to the rich and famous?" the little monk asked in return. He noted her seriousness. It was time for him to open the narrow gate to the cross.

"You need to die fully to self, to be crucified with Christ, as the apostle Paul teaches. You need to give your life to God voluntarily and without any reservations whatsoever. You must surrender all and then all will be given to you. Seek first the kingdom of God and many of these other issues will be settled for you.

"What's really holding you back?" the little monk asked further.

With great difficulty the woman confessed, "I have a fear of putting my life totally in the hands of God." At this confession, the little monk swallowed hard. "God is love," he replied softly.

"But it's so hard," said the woman.

"Fénelon said that 'a cross carried in simplicity, without the interference of self adding to the weight of it, is not really so bad,'" answered the little monk.

"Won't all this just lead to constant grinding away of my mind on these things, just as I have been doing in the past?"

the woman asked in desperation. "I'm so weary of analyzing my soul."

"The way of the cross says No," the little monk answered. "Introspection? No. Ruminating? No. Endless striving? No. Restless pondering? No. But peace of mind and heart? Yes. Crucified with Christ once for all time. Yes! This is the ultimate Yes.

"Let me share with you this prayer of Søren Kierkegaard:

> 'Teach me, O God,
>> not to torture myself
>> not to make a martyr out of myself
>>> through stifling reflection,
>>> but rather teach me to breathe deeply
>>> in faith.'"

The woman, looking disheveled in all her fine clothes, pulled a lace handkerchief from her lap and wept her way the final distance to the cross. The agony of surrender and the difficulty of repentance were real, but so was the victory. Darkness fell away. Peace flowed from the deepest well. Joy. Fire. Love. The face of God. The utter freshness of deep down things.

If only Gorbon Kreeg had seen the things that this woman of wealth has seen, thought the little monk.

After a time of simple fellowship in the garden, the little monk teased the woman into swinging on the garden gate. Soon, Purr joined them, swinging her head back and forth in rhythm with the gate.

The woman stayed for several weeks, receiving much of the teaching the little monk had to offer. Their hours together were often filled with hearty laughter. He showed her the well where he often prayed. He took her to Prophets' Point and showed her the oak and its sturdiness, the evergreen and its message of ongoing life, and the holly and its promise of victory through suffering. They went down the path called King's Highway to the shepherd's house for dinner. Sometimes they would join the children of the village in a game of hide and seek.

The days passed all too quickly. The little monk found himself waving good-bye to a gracious trophy in God's gallery of redeemed souls. She left in all her fine clothes, but her heart wore sackcloth and ashes.

She reminded him in many ways of his mother. For several weeks after the woman's visit, the little monk thought often of his mother. He remembered his mother telling him each morning, "Go do something beautiful today. Make God proud of you." His lingering thoughts of his mother led him to a decision: He would build a new well for his mother, a monument in memory of her.

Others offered to help dig, but the stonework was something he wanted to do alone. For a whole summer he carried stones from the river to Prophets' Point.

Often from the hill above, the shepherd would watch and wait with interest and admiration.

The little monk did not mind the sharp pain caused by this hard work. He took each stone to the edge of the meadow to build the well.

Then, one day, toward evening, just before winter, near the time of the coming of the moon, he finished the well. The little monk lifted his eyes to survey the wide meadow. He inhaled the wind and turned his heart to contemplation. He closed his eyes to grasp more firmly the wideness of God's mercy. How vast the kingdom of God is, he thought, as his soul poured out its gratitude for the seventh gift that had saved him from Gorbon Kreeg.

The little monk looked at the sky and studied an evening cloud, a puffy crimson one, all aglow from the setting sun.

He sketched the cloud in his journal and named the cloud, "Bountiful."

He turned from this scene to gather some logs a short distance away.

Purr lay in the grass to feel the wind blow across her fur. Tiring of this, she began to play with a hazelnut, rolling it between her paws. Suddenly, she flipped the hazelnut too hard with her paw and it flew into the air and down the well. When it splashed in the water at the bottom of the well, it made a soft echo, so that the little monk heard behind him what seemed to be a murmur on the wind. He heard words so silent only the heart could hear them: "Jesus is Lord."

The little monk turned back to the well to see if anyone was there, but the meadow was empty, except for two solitary rabbits sniffing the ground in search of autumn leftovers.

He took Purr in his arms and looked up at the crimson, evening sky, disturbed only by a soft mellow moon emerging. "Mother, this deepest of wells is for you," he whispered.

The next day, early in the morning, he gathered more logs to build around the well a wooden fence—and a narrow gate.

"He took Purr in his arms…"